Your Aging Parents

Your Aging Parents

by John Deedy

THE THOMAS MORE PRESS
Chicago, Illinois

Acknowledgements

Material in the section "Aged and With You" is recast, with permission, from an article in *Charities USA* (November, 1982) by Sister Nancy Vendura, D.C.

Chapter 9 reproduces with minor stylistic changes sections of *A Family Handbook on Alzheimer's Disease and Related Disorders* of the Behavioral Neurology Unit at Boston's Beth Israel Hospital, and these appear here with permission.

Gratitude is also expressed to Claretian Publications of Chicago for permission to recycle some material from *Generation,* a newsletter for aging and aged Catholics, of which the author of this book is editor.

ISBN 0-88347-160-4

Contents

For Kristine and Tara

OUR GREYING SOCIETY
AN INTRODUCTION

WHEN Steve Allen, the entertainer and writer, turned 61, he congratulated himself in a *Center Magazine* interview for not feeling a day above 50. Indeed, he was almost ecstatic about his age. True, he did not feel like a kid anymore, and he conceded that he could not get on a bike now and pedal it up a hill. But what the heck! When he was a kid, all his uncles "were dying, or were already dead" by age 60.

Allen's point was personal, but at the same time it dramatized one of the astonishing social developments of the second half of the 20th Century: People are living longer, much longer. In 1789, life expectancy in the United States was about 34 years. How changed the picture! A baby born in the United States in 1982 can expect to live 74.5 years, according to projections of the Metropolitan Life Insurance Company.

Take it from another angle. In 1900 there were only 3 million Americans who were 65 years of age or older, and they comprised only 4 percent of the population. Today, that percentage stands at 11.3, with 25.5 million Americans being 65 or older. People are living longer everywhere in the world except for East Asia. More precisely, many more are living the maximum life-span. This is especially so in the United States. In 1980 persons attaining age 65 had an average life expectancy of an additional 16.4 years. Women, who live longer than men on the average, could expect to live an additional 18.4 years; men, 14.1 years. Those figures project to a life expectancy of 83.4 for women who attain age 65, and 79.1 years for men. Steve Allen's uncles should have been so lucky.

Once upon a time it was not a very pleasant thing to grow old. In one far-away society the elderly were expected to steal off into the night when they became frail . . . there to die, and by their dying make room for a member of the new generation. In another, a family stone was kept which would be "mercifully" dropped on the head of the old person when age translated to uselessness. Today things are more humane, and on the whole have been so for millennia, despite scandalous lapses into barbarism on occasion by nations and political regimes. They are humane in the United States.

To be sure, many elderly Americans slip through the so-cial-service safety nets, and live precarious existences on bare incomes or by wits alone. On the other hand, there is that other segment of the elderly, the vast majority, for whom these are, if not the best of times, then certainly not the worst. The Reagan administration commented not long ago that older Americans are the "wealthiest, best-fed, best-housed, healthiest, most self-reliant older population in our history." In a definite sense they are. Ninety-five percent of the older population is covered by Medicare; an overwhelmingly large percentage is sufficient unto itself; and as Ronald B. Stuckey, executive director of the Wart-burg Lutheran Home for the Aging in Brooklyn, New York, has pointed out, less than 5 percent of the elderly— one out of 20 old persons on a given day—requires institu-tionalization. Further, it is estimated that up to 40 percent of these institutionalized elderly could remain in their com-

munities if organized care-support facilities were available
—or utilized.

This happy state is not, however, without its complications, particularly for the middle generation of Americans.
Before full longevity became a commonplace for such vast
numbers of people, the average middle-aged American
couple could look forward to their own old age as a time, if
not of absolute comfort, then at least of leisure and of
freedom of responsibility for caring or worrying about
others than themselves. Their parents would be dead, and
their own children presumably would be settled into their
own family situations or careers as adult singles, so that
that 20- or 30-year burden of having to raise and guide and
supervise would be blessedly ended. But longevity has
changed all that. Today, the three- and four-generational
family is the rule of American society, and couples in their
50s, 60s, and even 70s are finding that they have shed one
responsibility only to be confronted by another: their aged
parents. The ones who raised them are now the ones who
need them—in different ways and varying degrees, of
course. Whatever one might be able to say about the independence of the modern grandparent, for many adult
children dependency roles have been reversed. They must
now care for those who once cared for them.

The changes in family structure and function during this
century have been startling. Though more dispersed, the
multigenerational family is as common now as the com-
puter, 70 percent of Americans aged 65 or older being
grandparents and 40 percent being great-grandparents.
The average age at which women and men today become
grandparents is 54 and 57, respectively. Why, their own
parents are probably in their mid- or latter-70s, which is

hardly decrepitude any longer. That toddler who 50 years ago was lucky to know a grandparent, probably knows all four today, and a great-grandparent or two in the bargain.

What are the implications of this social phenomenon spawned by improved science, better health care, and advancing educational and social welfare programs that enable more and more persons to achieve the maximum of potential years? More specifically, what are the challenges and problems for those who must deal with the fact of aged parents? What are they likely to be called upon to deal with, to cope with?

These are extraordinarily large questions that defy easy textbooks answers, for as Laurence G. Branch and Alan M. Jette of the Division of Aging at Harvard University Medical School make clear, the dependency of aged persons varies markedly from person to person, and even from gender to gender. Women, for instance, are much more likely than men to need help in performing basic activities of daily living (assistance in walking, transfers, dressing, bathing, eating, and grooming), while men are more likely to need more assistance than women in instrumental activities of daily living (assistance in housekeeping, transportation, food preparation, grocery shopping, and personal business affairs). Such is the conclusion offered by Branch and Jette on the basis of a sampling of 1,625 noninstitutionalized Massachusetts residents aged 65 or older.

Further, Branch and Jette found that dependency in activities of daily living increased in direct relation to age. Thus, whereas 80 percent of the total sampling were entirely self-sufficient in performing basic activities of daily living, when Branch and Jette studied those 85 and older, they found that 42 percent required help in basic activities of daily living, and 99 percent in instrumental activities of daily living.

To some, all this might seem like sociological frittering, except that it is essential that we know what older persons are capable of, at least within some broad spectrum. As Branch and Jette comment, "The capacity to perform basic activities of daily living, as well as instrumental activities of daily living, is crucial to an elder's ability to maintain himself or herself in the community. The ability to prepare food is as important as the ability to dress, if an elder is to remain outside the confines of a long-term care institution."

The point of the Branch-Jette study is related primarily to public policy. The Harvard sociologists argue that "if our society is genuinely committed to trying to meet the long-term care needs of the aging population in the least restrictive environment, we must increase the government role in supporting social services that many elders need to maintain themselves in their home environment." Likewise, they maintain that "differences between men and women in the sample serve to remind us that policies and programs often need to be tailored differently for older women than for older men."

Yet, though the study may concern public-policy makers in the main, it is of direct interest to adult children with aged parents, both for its emphases on community living (as distinct from institutional living) and for the challenges, to use that word again, which it presents to adult children to be more than loving, caring offspring, but also to be amateur para-sociologists of a sort. For as parents age, adult children are inevitably going to be more and more tested. For 40 years or more it may have seemed to the children that their parents never changed. But now, suddenly the changes are dramatic and sudden, between 65 and 70, between 71 and 74, between 75 and 84. The adult child is the first to have to deal with this, and it is important that he or she have some notion of what to expect and how to react.

Such is the purpose of this book. It does not give all the answers; it does not raise all the questions. Rather, it outlines some problem areas and proposes courses of action, often by way of case studies. If it proves useful to readers, it will be because my research and my experiences with two remarkably self-sufficient parents in their 80s persuade me that the topics broached here are typical of what the adult child is called upon to face. I should add that four years as editor of *Generation,* a Claretian Publications newsletter for middle-aged and aged Catholics, have also produced insights which I trust will be of value. Unless otherwise stated, names used in case studies have been changed.

John Deedy
Rockport, Massachusetts

Chapter 1

ADULT CHILDREN

That Increasingly Common Species

LET'S open on a note of realism: Whatever the impressions that might be conveyed by beaming senior citizens boarding buses to Disneyland or teeing up on palm-lined Florida golf courses, aging is not a fun thing. Growing old translates to loss: loss of figure, of looks, of strength, of job, of close friends, of old enjoyments. Some people age like a good wine, and do great things with their old age. Goethe completed *Faust* at age 82; Luigi Cornaro at 95 demonstrated how Venice could reclaim its wasteland. But aging is not an exciting adventure for everyone, and it is particularly not exciting for that increasingly large number of people who must face the fact of their own aging at the same time that they are made aware that dependency roles are reversed with respect to their parents. Thus, they approach their own retirement with the prospect that those who did for them in their youth now are in, or approaching, a stage in life where they must be cared for, or guided, or helped in one way or several. For the middle-aged, the adult child, and the elderly, the aged parent, it is a chancy time in the life cycle, and those annoyingly up-beat journals about aging do a disservice to romanticize the complications out of existence.

"Getting old is pure hell," remarks Ruth M. Snow of Baltimore, Maryland. "Aging in itself strips you of your independence, which in turn results in losing your dignity, your self-esteem, and everything else. All you need to do is visit a 'nursing home' or a 'home for the aged,' and no other explanations are needed. I have seen them all, and indeed they are depressing.''

Mrs. Snow speaks with authority. She retired at age 55, after working 36 years for the Government as an administrative secretary. "I retired so that I could stay at home and take care of my mother, who was then 81 years of age,'' she explains. "She could not be left alone due to 'dementia.' There is no way my mother could live alone and on her own. Her Social Security check is $196.04 per month. She lives with me, and I take care of her. If she didn't have me, I can't imagine what would happen to her. Knowing the world as it is today, they would probably warehouse her in a mental institution. I am glad I am able to take care of her, and I pray to God every day that nothing happens to me through accident or terminal illness.''

What does it mean to have parents growing old and frail? To different people, it means different things. Mrs. Snow looks at her mother, and she sees herself in the future. "Quite frankly it scares me to death,'' she exclaims. It is a common reaction. Very many middle-aged persons look at their parents, and it is as if they were looking into a mirror at their own aging and mortality. Still it is only one of many possible reactions. Another is the reaction alluded to earlier: the worry of having to assume new responsibility at the very time when one's own needs due to aging are increasing. Or of guilt, real or imagined, for relationships of the past or present, involving one's parents.

John and Mary Downey felt a certain familial guilt after his job took him 800 miles distant from his parents. Under badgering from a sister-in-law, who complained constantly about her and her husband having to carry the full load of the aged parents, largely emotional, the Downeys moved back to within 50 miles of his parents. They discovered that 50 miles might as well be 1500 miles, and that the sister-in-law was only playing the role of the martyr anyway. The Downeys' guilt was imagined, and it was complicated by the pressure brought by the sister-in-law. They would have been better off staying where they were.

As the Downeys felt guilt, others feel sadness—for themselves, or parents who were once so self-sufficient and are now so dependent. Or they feel hostility, because suddenly, they are burdened at the very moment in life when they looked forward to being free. Reactions can run the range of behavioral possibilities.

How does one sort them out?

First, by understanding what is happening in the broad society and appreciating that you're not alone in what is happening to you. About four-fifths of older people have at least one surviving adult child, according to Elaine M. Brody, director of the Department of Human Services at the Philadelphia Geriatric Center. So the adult child with aged parents is anything but a unique specimen. There are a lot of them out there, including married couples, very many of whom can count four very old parents between them. Nearly one-fourth of those 58- to 59-years-old have a surviving parent, while 10 percent of those between ages 58 and 63 have both parents living.

That makes obvious the second step: Reach out and communicate with other adult children. Some persons might be able to go it alone, but it is a whole lot easier when problems are shared, challenges sorted out, and remedies exchanged. It is hard to beat group experience, particularly small group experience. People need one another, and they are better off sharing experiences, listening, hearing, giving and receiving emotional support. Thus, in Washtenaw County, Michigan, there is APGO ("As Parents Grow Older"), a Child and Family Service, Inc., program formed to assist families to learn about the aging process, to become knowledgeable about available communuity services, to explore strategies in response to individual problems, and to share personal feelings. Similar programs exist or are in the process of being formed elsewhere. The challenge for the individual is to locate them—or bring them into being, if need be. In either instance, it is not a daunting challenge. To locate an adult-child support group might only require a telephone call to a local social services agency; to form one might only require two adult children coming together and discussing common problems.

Supporting One's Parents

What does an adult child owe an aging parent?

Legally, the answer to that question is in contention. In 1983 the Reagan administration, in a new interpretation of the Medicaid law, informed state officials that they may require people to help pay for the care provided to their parents in nursing homes. In so acting Washington was reflecting a policy that is already operative in scattered places. Some 26 states have long-standing laws on their books that require children to contribute to the support of their needy parents, according to Daniel Callahan, director of the Hastings Center, a research organization which focuses on ethics in the life sciences, medicine, and the professions.

The idea of family responsibility for aged parents is not a recent legal concept. The English Poor Law of 1601 spelled out the then-radical principle that society should be responsible for the poor, but, pulling back the hand of relief that had just been extended, the law also stated that public funds were not to be expended until the family's private resources had been exhausted. As Callahan notes, the ostensible rationale behind the requirement of family support was the biblical injunction to honor one's father and mother—the Fourth Commandment, it will be recalled. However, historians are pretty much agreed that the real reason for the proviso was to protect the public treasury.

Whatever the history of "family responsibility" the Reagan administration directive, channeled through the Department of Health and Human Services, touched off an animated debate on the role of the government in enforcing filial responsibility.

Those favoring the concept, such as the American Health Care Association, see enforcement of filial responsibility conserving Medicaid funds for those most in need. "With Federal Medicaid funds being reduced and states finding it difficult to adequately finance their Medicaid programs, family financial responsibility concepts should be considered," the association said in its statement. Similarly, Patrick Nipp, president of the National Council of Health Centers, commented that a "family responsibility" law would encourage family members to participate in decisions about the care of an elderly relative. "They will visit their relative more frequently to assure that he or she is receiving the necessary services," he added.

But others are not so sure. Elma L. Holder, of the National Citizens' Coalition for Nursing Home Reform, is one of them. "The children of those in nursing homes are often themselves in their 60s and nearing retirement," she said to the *New York Times*. "Will people on fixed incomes now be expected to pay for their parents' institutional care? How will the burden be divided among family members of different means, and among relatives who live in different states?" Others wonder whether a married person will be required to support his or her in-law parent. Apart from the details of implementation, Cynthia Rudder of the Nursing Home Community Coalition of New York State comments that the potential saving to government is "insignificant compared with the financial and psychological stress that will be placed on both the nursing home resident and his or her adult children."

The most cogent objection, however, is Callahan's. "The only basis for declaring a legal obligation would be that of a contracted debt that children owe parents," he said on the *Times'* op-ed page. "But whatever the nature of the filial bond, it is not that. To attempt to save public money by capitalizing on the parent-child bond only compounds the error. It uses the state's power to introduce a threat to the integrity of relationships between generations."

Does it follow then that the adult child owes his aging parents nothing? Of course not. At the very least, the adult child owes parents debts of gratitude and affection, and in any healthy child-parent relationship this will be a felt obligation, which in turn will motivate caring in direct ways.

If government feels it must be doing something, then let it follow Callahan's advice. Let it provide attractive incentives to families to provide care for their elderly members. Despite what some bureaucrats may think, adult children are most reluctant to place their aging parent(s) in a nursing home. In the overwhelming number of instances, the nursing home is the last, not the first recourse of families with problems involving aged parents. One of the ennobling things about our society is that adult children already do a great deal for their parents—by way of time, attention, affection, and help of sundry kind. As Callahan says, there is reason to believe they would be receptive to programs designed to reduce costs by voluntarily enlisting their help even more. But to make aged-parent responsibility a matter of law would only lead to dilemmas and conflicts, administrative and intergenerational, alongside which those presently existing would be insignificant.

Thus, back to the opening question of this section: What does an adult child owe an aging parent? In point of law, nothing—or at least very little. But in point of gratitude and affection, everything—certainly in those families where love has flowed between the generations in both directions since the years when those who are now old were young, and those who are adult children were mere babes. Happily, this seems to be the vast majority of families in our country, whatever the very real problems and intergenerational differences.

If You're Different, So Are Your Parents

There is scarcely a parent who has not grappled at one time or another with the generation gap between him or her and the young ones of the family. Indeed, it has been a common familial exercise since the 1960s. What is not always realized, however, is that a generation gap can also develop between adult children, those of the second generation, and the parents who raised them, those of the third generation. Indeed, the generation gap between the second and third generations can be much more pronounced, much more difficult to cope with than a second-first generation gap, because the gap has very probably been broadened by time and distance. The rearing of one's own family, the passing of a quarter-century, the probability that one's occupation had taken one hundreds of miles from the old home town—factors such as those can make strangers of a sort out of people who were once tightly knit under the one roof. Drawn back together by circumstances of aging and familial responsibilities, the parents one thought one knew may be as strange, as hard to understand as one's own children sometimes seem to be.

Nothing of this should surprise the adult child. The tendency is to remember one's parents exactly as they were when they were in the rearing years, and you were being reared. But they evolve too, and by the time they are ensconced as members of the third generation, they may be quite different from the parents you knew as a child.

Tom M. grew up in a house where the mother was the so-called Rock of Gibralter. She managed the finances, was the primary rearer and guider of the children, shaped the major decisions of the family, and kept the father on a straight though not always narrow path. Tom returned after living for years in another part of the country to find that the mother had soured on life and her role in the household. Her children's success had become her husband's failure. She complained constantly, lost interest in shopping and cooking, and had donned the mantle of martyr. The father assumed roles that once were hers. He was now the responsible one.

Tom's is an experience that every adult child should realize could be theirs. Despite what the adage might say, people do not become set in old age. They are evolving like the rest of humanity, often in unpredictable ways, some of them loving, maybe some of them aggravating. Most certainly, one's parents at 75 are not the parents one remembers from 40 years ago. They are as different as one is one-self, and this can necessitate a whole new set of rules for a happy and satisfying relationship, a whole new methodology for the love that translates to responsible care and devotion. The adult child is challenged to become amateur psychologist, provider maybe, decision maker—if the reversal of roles has become complete.

No two human or family situations will be the same, but there is one constant: The needs of those of the older generation do not differ appreciably from those of any other. As psychologist Barbara Silverstone has remarked, "Old people need love, affection, sexual contact, a roof over their heads, food in their mouths, decent medical care, help when they are sick or disabled, and the need to feel good about themselves (self-esteem)." Some aging parents will insist on maintaining lifelong patterns of activity; some may lapse into passivity. Still, whatever the pattern of behavior, the needs are those of people of any other generation, distinguished of course by degree. An older person, for instance, is likely to require more medical care than someone who is young.

In sum, adult children assessing (or reassessing) filial responsibility with respect to aging parents should be aware from the start that the parents of old age will be different, psychologically as well as physically, from the parents who nurtured them years before. Aging does things to people, which is why an understanding of one's own aging is vital to the process of understanding one's aged parents.

Coming to Terms with One's Own Aging

In 1891, when Oliver Wendell Holmes, the New England poet, novelist, essayist, and physician, was 82 years old, he received a letter from a man in Chester County, Pennsylvania, discussing the merits of longevity. Holmes wrote back:

> My dear friend,
>
> The age you accuse yourself of—shall I not say rather congratulate yourself upon—does not seem so advanced to me, who am almost ten years ahead of it.
>
> One lesson I have learned, and I doubt not that you also have learned it. *Every decade has lessons of its own which it alone can teach us.* You are wiser in some things than you were or could be at sixty. So it will be when you are eighty—ninety or a hundred—if you live so long. May you fill out your century of life, if you desire to, and get that last lesson which only centenarians live long enough to learn.
>
> Yours sincerely,
Oliver Wendell Holmes

Holmes' point is incontestable. Every decade has lessons of its own to impart, but most of us, particularly in our near-middle and middle years, block out the reality of our own aging. Notice how we resist decadal birthdays as if they were some kind of fearful omen, a death sentence of sorts. I know a woman who sat down in the middle of the living room floor and cried on her 29th birthday, because next year she would be 30. Not this year; *next* year. It was pretty silly, except this was a few years ago, and she did belong to the generation that believed in not trusting anyone over 30. Of course she recovered from her distress—that very night even, after my wife and I, who were 15 years older, were called by her anxious husband to come and share a store-bought birthday cake and prove by our presence that life can be worth living at 45 as well as at 30.

The generational distance between me and my friends is not so great as between children and their parents, yet that birthday experience dramatizes a problem common to most adult child/older-parent relationships: there is a chasm of understanding, at times, because the adult child is unreconciled to the fact of his or her own aging. Parents get older and older; the child stays the same. At least half of the equation is self-delusional, and what difficulties that can cause in intergenerational associations!

Thus a basic principle in second-generation/third-generation relations: to realize and understand better what is happening to one's older parent it is absolutely essential that one be aware of the fact of one's own aging. Otherwise, the distance between the two generations will be as nothing compared to the generation-gap that sociologists of the 1960s used to speak of between the first and second generations of those turbulent times.

The young, of course—like my 29-year-old friend— think that they are never going to grow old. It is one of the grand deceptions of the sunny years. But people in the middle generation should know better, for the reality of aging is all over them—in muscles that ache after mild exercise, in greying and thinning hair, in lost molars. Yet middle-aged people are frequently as blind as young folks to the fact of aging, and this creates an understanding block that extends from the family to the broader society. Father Henri Nouwen of the Yale Divinity School noticed it, and made these observations in *Church Leaders Bulletin/A.D. 1981:*

"To receive the elderly into our inner self . . . is far from easy. Old age is hidden not just from our eyes, but much more from our feelings. In our deepest self we keep living with the illusion that we will always be the same. We not only tend to deny the real existence of old men and women living in their closed rooms and nursing homes, but also the old man and woman who is slowly awakening in our own center. They are strangers, and strangers are fearful. They are intruders threatening to rob us of what we consider our own. Care for the elderly means, first of all, to make ourselves available to the experiences of becoming old. . . . Caring is first a way to our own aging self, where we can find the healing powers for all those who share in the human condition.''

Some, such as Rabbi Sanford Seltzer of the Union of American Hebrew Congregations in Brookline, Massachusetts, advise the creation of mechanisms whereby persons in middle age have an opportunity to discuss openly their feelings about growing older, thereby coming to terms with this inexorable reality. Indeed, at Temple Israel in Boston, precisely such an opportunity exists as part of an aging awareness program that Temple Israel has developed for its membership. One segment of the program is entitled "My Parents and I Are Changing and Aging," and is designed as an intergenerational experience enabling families to focus on the dynamics of aging and how these changes affect familial relationships.

Such programs are wonderful. However, they are not within the availability of everyone geographically, for it is the rare community that has the imagination, the means, and the personnel to sponsor in any broad way a program like Temple Israel's. On the other hand, there is common sense. Aging is the one inescapable fact in all our lives, and we should take stock of it. Those of us who fail to, those of us who are blind to the fact of our own aging, will never understand the aging problems of our aged parents.

Rather, we will be creating a latter-life generational gap between ourselves and our parents. But recognition depends for effectiveness on a certain familiarity with the changes and processes that are taking place in the two generational groups. We are not called individually to be professional gerontologists, but it is incumbent on each of us to have understanding and knowledge of a general gerontological kind. This is easily come by in any public library by checking the books listed under the card-catalogue heading of Aging. A little research there will eliminate many problems of understanding before they even arise.

Let me recommend a few titles:

Butler, Robert N., *Why Survive? Being Old in America.* New York: Harper & Row, 1975.

Silverstone, Barbara, and Hyman, Helen Kandel, *You and Your Aging Parent: The Modern Family's Guide to Emotional, Physical, and Financial Problems.* New York: Pantheon, 1976, 1982.

Kübler-Ross, Elisabeth, *On Death and Dying.* New York: Macmillan, 1969.

Lester, Andrew D., and Lester, Judith L., *Understanding Aging Parents.* Philadelphia: Westminster, 1980.

Ragan, Pauline K., ed., *Aging Parents.* Los Angeles: University of Southern California, 1978.

Harris, Charles S., research coordinator, *Fact Book on Aging: A Profile of America's Older Population.* Washington: The National Council on the Aging, Inc., 1978.

Shanas, Ethel, and Streib, Gordon, eds., *Social Structures and the Family: Generational Relations.* Englewood Cliffs, N.J.: Prentice-Hall, 1965.

De Beauvoir, Simone, *The Coming of Age.* New York: Putnam's, 1972.

Deeken, Alfons, *Growing Old, and How to Cope With It.* Ramsey, N.J.: Paulist/Newman Press, 1972.

Fritz, Dorothy B., *Growing Old Is a Family Affair.* Atlanta, John Knox Press, 1972.

Galton, Lawrence N., *Don't Give Up on an Aging Parent.* New York, Crown, 1975.

.

Chapter 2

THE EXTENDED FAMILY

Beware Overdoses of "TLC"

THE instinct in every loyal child is to be generous and kind to the parents. After all, the child owes to the parents the most precious of gifts—life itself. This generosity and kindness take many forms throughout life, and as the years advance often merge into what the hip call TLC, "tender loving care." A little TLC is good for everyone, but, to paraphrase what the Food and Drug Administration says about some consumer products, too much TLC can be hazardous to health. In older persons, it could subtly lead to an erroneous belief that they are incompetent, and this in turn could have extremely deleterious physical and psychological effects on the aged person.

Dr. Ellen J. Langer, professor of psychology at Harvard University, and Dr. Jerry Avorn, director of the program in geriatrics at Harvard University School of Public Health and assistant professor of preventive and social medicine at Harvard University Medical School, confirm this. "Because the elderly as a group are seen as frail and vulnerable, the tendency of society in general is to treat them with special care—always being ready to 'help the little old lady across the street.'" The impulse may be mistaken, they argue. "Simply helping people may make them incompetent," Langer and Avorn declare. "While well-meaning, it communicates to the person that the person is not able to do whatever it is for himself or herself. If the person faces no difficultly, if there are no challenges, large or small, feelings of mastery are precluded and consequences like involution, depression, and premature death are real possibilities rather than mere exaggeration."

Langer tells of a study which she and Professor Judith Rodin, of Yale University, conducted among an elderly group of nursing home residents, the purpose of which was to test the importance of aged persons feeling more control and responsibility for day-to-day events. Plants were used. One group was offered plants to care for themselves, while the other group was given plants that were watered by the staff. Beforehand, the nursing home administrator delivered a talk to the residents. He emphasized to the former group their responsibility for themselves, whereas the communication to the latter group stressed the staff's responsibility for them as patients.

The results were astonishing. Residents in the responsibility-induced group became more active and reported feeling happier than the comparison group of residents, who were encouraged to feel that the staff would care for them and try to make them happy. Residents in the responsibility-induced group also showed a significant improvement in alertness and increased behavioral involvement in many different kinds of activities, such as movie attendance, active socializing with staff and friends, and contest participation.

By way of another example, Langer and Avorn comment that helping a nursing home resident to get dressed to go to breakfast (either out of concern for the resident or to save time for the staff) may only result "in feelings of incompetence and dependence for the resident and ultimately take more of the staff's time since the individual will soon come to assume the need for such help."

True, the Langer-Avorn and Langer-Rodin reports relate to nursing home environments, but as Langer and Avorn state in their paper (published as a chapter in *Congregate Housing for Older People,* J. Seagle and R. Chellis, editors, Lexington, 1981), what is true in nursing homes is true in the wider society. The instinct to overprotect may take other forms, and it may originate from altogether different reasons, but it is there nonetheless.

The message, obviously, is to beware of doing too much for aged parents who are capable of managing for themselves. Chances are that their alertness, happiness, active participation in life, and general sense of well-being will be better served if they have perceived control of their lives. Of course if the parents are unable to manage or cope, that is another matter, but when that time comes, the aged parents themselves will know it, and generally they will speak out to let the adult child know what kind of help is needed, and precisely how much of that help. The wise adult child will be guided by the parents' wishes—and maybe keep a wary eye open at the same time, just in case the aged parents minimize the help they need.

Noble Intentions Can Be Fatal

A particular time of temptation for intruding unnecessarily into one's parent's life is when the mother or father has become widowed.

Harry M.'s father died in his mid-70s. The mother, a few years younger, was left alone, but she was healthy and content. She lived in a very pleasant neighborhood, near sisters and a flock of nieces and nephews. She had been left well provided for financially by her husband, and presumably she would be looked in on regularly by kinfolk. But the son felt a special responsibility about having the mother with him, and so, under his prodding, she moved several hundred miles to be with the son and his family. At first it was an adventure for the aged parent, but as time lengthened and the realization set in that this was not a long visit, but a permanent relocation, a new world to adjust to, the mother seemed to lose some of her spark. She grew apathetic and lost interest in her surroundings. Coincidentally, her health deteriorated, and death mercifully relieved her of her unhappiness.

At the wake, the aunts and cousins congratulated Harry on being such a loving and protective child, saying such things as, wasn't he lucky that he had his mother with him at the end. Well, Harry was lucky. On the other hand, it just may be that with all his good intentions he weakened the mother by becoming overly protective of her.

In *The Ann Landers Encyclopedia A to Z,* Dr. Robert N. Butler, director of the National Institute of Aging in Bethesda, Maryland, remarked from 20-plus years of clinical and research observation on "a common tendency to underestimate the capacities of our older people." Very possibly our renamed but not mythical Harry underestimated the capacities of his mother; most certainly he failed to take into account the psychological and physical disturbance that abrupt geographical dislocation can cause in an older person, particularly one who has never traveled much heretofore. Some older persons adjust very well to geographical relocation, but for others it can be a very debilitating experience, and adult children should be aware of the possibility before they make a decision about yanking parents from their old environment.

As Butler commented, "It is crucial that we encourage our parents and older relatives to become or to remain self-starters." Which is to say, don't take over their lives. It is important that they have as much control over their lives as possible. As you should not kill them with kindness, neither should you kill them with noble intentions.

The problem is, of course, that many older persons do not forever remain self-starters. Their health goes, their mind slips, they grow frail, and the adult child has no recourse but to step in and with the parent make some difficult decisions about the parent's future. Maybe this will involve nursing home placement, about which more in chapter 8. But until that day when one's aged parent cannot fend for herself or himself, the adult child is advised to let the aged parent manage his or her own life. This is not to say that the adult child should be indifferent or neglectful. It is only to say that adult children should not smother the initiative and the will of aged parents to do for themselves.

Reuniting The Family

The relationship of grandparents to their adult children and to the grandchildren has always been a sensitive issue. Certainly it was in those yesterdays when almost as a matter of tradition three generations lived under the one roof. The temptation must have been forever strong for the generations to intrude on one another—grandparents, for instance, lingering in a parenting role with children who have been adults long since; adult children assuming responsibilities and prerogatives that the grandparents still considered theirs; grandchildren wondering where the primary family authority rested, particularly in households where grandparents intruded into the raising of the grandchildren, a proclivity as enduring as the ages, it sometimes seems.

The three-generation household pretty much went the

way of the horse-and-buggy with Social Security (which has enabled many older people to live independently and on their own terms), the disappearance of the family farm, job migration, and the building boom that followed World War II, when small homes could be acquired by young couples at very cheap mortgage rates. But these are different days, and the three-generation household is becoming common once again, as longevity, to say nothing of a changing economy, characterized by high rents, high taxes, high food costs, high cost of everything, forces the generations back under the one roof in increasingly large numbers. About 20 percent of aged parents now live with their adult children.

Almost any aged-parent/adult-child living arrangement has its drawbacks, but if any adult child is unhappy about the prospect of an aged parent moving in, whether blood parent or in-law, let him or her know that the parent likely isn't happy about it either. Studies show that elderly parents cherish their independence just as much as adult children do. If some adult children are reluctant about entering into a co-living arrangement with their parents, chances are that the parents are no less reluctant. Having led their own lives for 60 or 70 or 80 years, they would prefer continuing to do so. In addition, many older persons are sensitive about being burdens to their children, with respect either to health or finances.

Yet the arrangement need not be burdensome—unless, of course, the aged parent is physically incompetent or is unwilling to do things around the house. In most instances, however, aged parents welcome responsibilities. They want to have something to do. It gives them a sense of belonging, of participating, of being part of the family picture. For Mother, maybe it is the preparation of the main meal two or three days a week; for Dad, maybe it is the weeding of the garden and the tending of the tomato patch. The responsibilities should be mutually agreed upon, so that no one will feel that he or she is being saddled with an onerous chore. Responsibilites should be reviewed on occasion, and it goes without saying that those assumed should be faithfully met.

Consider All the Consequences

Bringing aged parents into the house to live has a strong sentimental element about it, but the adult child is advised not to be too sentimental or impulsive in arriving at a decision. The adult child should be quite certain that moving in together is what he or she really wants and is what is best for the whole family, including the aged parent. A father, for instance, who never got along with his son hitherto in life is not likely to get along with him in the dependency of old age, and this circumstance could make for a very abrasive situation within the son's household if the father moved in. It could put a strain on the son's equanimity, his marriage, perhaps his relations with his own children. Counselors advise, therefore, the examination of cold, careful questions beforehand. Specifically:

• How does your spouse feel about your aged parent's moving in?

• Is there really enough living space, or will you be crawling up and down one another's back?

• Will the move-in change your lives, devastate your privacy, make it impossible for you to entertain, lay on you a new and impossible dependency?

• How did you get along with one another in the past, and is this what you would like for the indefinite future?

These are tough questions, and there are scores more

like them. But they must be asked and answered honestly. Sometimes, the answers will suggest that the old folks would be better off with someone else in the family, or in a retirement community, or in a care facility of one sort or another. In instances of this sort, the adult child should not feel guilty. One does not *owe* an adult parent a place in the home. It is no automatic obligation, legal or moral. If it is clear that the imposed elderly parent is going to wreak havoc on a young family, or if it is clear that the best interests of the elderly parent will be served by some other living arrangement, then the decision should be no, and other possibilities should be explored. Maybe with several of the children sharing costs, it will be possible to keep the adult parent(s) in the old house or apartment. Maybe the aged parent should be in a nursing home. But wherever the aged parent should be, it is not necessarily in the adult child's home.

On the other hand, perhaps after thoughtful consultation it is decided, "Yes, this is where Mother or Dad, or both, belong." One can only say, "wonderful," and congratulate those making the decision on their unselfish love. For theirs is a decision that undoubtedly will require sacrifices which will increase as the years proceed.

Yet, however welcome the aged parents are in the adult child's household, it should not be overlooked that adjustments will be imposed on everyone in the now-expanded family. Love and affection can help, of course. So too, a measure of deference, and of self-discipline and cooperation. But everyone should be prepared to make adjustments, some of which might not be easy.

Rules for the Reunited

Sometimes the reunion of the generations under one roof is accomplished with great harmony, but even in the best of cases there are strains and tensions. How can these be minimized?

Thomas Fox, family therapist at the St. Louis Psychological Institute, has advice to offer to adults with families of their own, who are rejoined by aged parents:

• Remember that no matter how many years sons or daughters may have been on their own, and no matter how successful they may be in their own parenting roles, old family procedures may not have changed. Mom may still be a constant critic; Dad may still be a constant advice-dispenser. Adult children should expect it. (Older parents, on the other hand, should beware of indulging old idiosyncrasies.)

• Talk about resentment; discuss problems. (For instance, why not establish a regular time, maybe once a week or once a month, for the airing of problems and the floating of suggestions?)

• The elder parents may say that their offspring are grown up, but that does not necessarily mean that they believe it. Still, the elder parents cannot exert the same authority with a 30- or 40-year-old that they could with that son or daughter when he or she was a youngster. The elder parents should not expect to; the son or daughter should not let them. Nor should his or her spouse.

• Nevertheless, adult children should be tolerant. Offspring need to be flexible. It is unfair to expect parents to change too much.

• When grandchildren are involved, set clear rules about who is in charge and who does the parenting.

On occasion, the situation is reversed, and it is the adult children who move in with their parents. The reason might be loss of job, financial strain, or divorce. These are Fox's tips for the older parents to keep in mind:

• Determine the length of the offspring's stay. This need not be precise, but there should be some idea about future plans.

• Don't refuse money if the offspring insists on paying something. Otherwise, you are enforcing the notion that you are taking care of that child.

• Space permitting, privacy is important. Having lived on their own for some time, offspring are no doubt used to time alone and space apart.

• Share responsibilities so that no one is made to feel useless.

• Resist meddling.

Links to the Past

Caring for one's aged parents in one's own home is regarded by very many as something less than a gala experience and rather more as a debt, a duty, a responsibility, a social or religious obligation. On the other hand, caring for parents can be a wonderfully positive experience, and particularly if there are young children in the household. Catherine O'Connell wrote about such an experience in *U.S. Catholic:*

"Herein lies yet another advantage in giving a home to your parents: They can provide a sense of the past, of heritage, of continuity to our families. By their very presence they tell children that life didn't begin in 1970, that whole generations of their ancestors lived in the dawn of history before TV and electric can openers. Maybe kids can learn some things from their grandparents. They can hear that some years back, growing up didn't mean seeing R-rated movies and asking for the car keys. Maybe it meant leaving home and your family and getting on a boat and crossing the ocean all alone at the age of 16. Maybe they'll hear what it was like to live through a real depression or to fight in a world war. And maybe they won't listen or they won't learn anything. But at least they deserve the chance to hear first hand about their own history."

But maybe some grandparents cannot tell their grandchildren about the past. They are too deaf, or too sick, or too "senile." "Still children can still learn from them," O'Connell remarks. "They can learn to be patient. They can learn to care for Gram or Grandpa even if they can no longer say thank you. By watching their parents' good example, maybe children will, in 30 or 40 years, be a little more hesitant about packing Mom and Dad off to the solar-powered all electrically monitored aging persons' care facility."

There are other advantages in having grandparents under the family roof, or at least nearby and within close contact: they can provide a bridge between the young people of the family and their own parents. This can be especially true in an age when youthful alienation and rebellion against old values are so much a part of the coming-of-age rite of passage. Authority barriers do not intrude between grandparents and grandchildren in the same way that often they do between the young and their parents. As a result, grandparents are in a position to develop much closer relationships with the young people. An obvious danger is that the grandparents can become intrusive, butting noses into family affairs that are not properly theirs. But this is a danger that the sensitive person can guard against by reading the signals that emanate from any interpersonal relationship, then butting-out.

Should Grandparents Be Built-In Baby-Sitters?

An obvious advantage of the three-generation household is that it comes with built-in baby-sitters. This is a great convenience for the parents of young children, but it can be wearying and annoying to the grandparents, certainly if they are being presumed upon. Of course, if baby-sitting is part of the agreed living arrangement, that is one thing. But if the grandparents are being unfairly imposed upon, then that is something else. Grandparents should not be required to be on call any hour, any day, as if they were some 24-hour service machine. They have served their time, as it were, in raising their own children. They should strive to be cooperative, but they are not required to be slaves.

This raises some interesting possibilities. Do grandparents have *any* responsibility for their children's children? Concomitantly, do young married couples have *any* right to expect that their own parents be available as baby-sitters whenever they are needed?

The questions apply beyond as well as to the three-generation household, and they were addressed by Phyllis Gallagher, counseling supervisor at Catholic Family Service in the Diocese of Spokane, Washington, in an *Our Sunday Visitor* interview.

"Personally, I don't feel as though I have any obligation [to be a baby-sitter]," said Gallagher, a grandmother. "But I must admit I enjoy baby-sitting my grandchildren. I don't baby-sit all the time; my daughter who lives here calls on high-school girls, also. But sometimes after a week filled with people with lots of problems, there is nothing as refreshing as seeing those little kids. They can give me lots of joy, even when they're not at their best."

What then about young parents who would like to have more support from their own parents in caring for the children, but the grandparents have decided that they are through baby-sitting? Grandparents, for instance, who say, "We raised our kids, and it was an exhausting and thankless task, and we don't want to have anything else to do with it." There are many such people, and we must all know a few of them.

Gallagher responded that she would not want such grandparents spending much time with her children, and she is absolutely right. "Grandparents like that probably help out with the kids only out of a sense of duty and fear that if they don't take their grandchildren once in a while maybe their adult children won't like them anymore. What is really beautiful is if grandparents can offer such help out of love for their adult offspring and love for their grand-children, not out of a sense of duty."

By way of example of a happy intergenerational contact, she drew from her own family history:

"Years ago, I had to be confined to the hospital for a lengthy stay following surgery. Rather than call upon my brothers or sister, all of whom lived a long way from us, I called upon my father—who had by this time been a wid-ower for many years—to care for my children. He and an aunt of mine together took care of them for me. And I've always treasured what happened as a result. After that, my children wanted to spend as much time as they could with their grandfather.

"They would say, 'There is so much to learn from him, Mother. If I could just go and have a couple of weeks with him and work with him, it would be wonderful.' Then later my oldest son traveled a great distance in the middle of winter in order to attend his grandfather's funeral Mass, and delivered the eulogy. That says something, I think, about what can exist between grandparents and grand-children."

Shifting ground a bit, it is unfortunate that the delicate skills of grandparenting—of being an adult friend to aging parents, and, in the case of aging parents themselves, of being adult friends to their adult children and grandchildren—are not better understood, taught, or valued in our society. This makes the more welcome *Grandparents/ Grandchildren: The Vital Connection,* a book by Arthur Kornhaber and Kenneth L. Woodward (Doubleday, 1981). The book points up the wonder of grandparenting, and demonstrates how rich a resource it can be for all the generations, when sensitively developed and made operative between the generations. If there is any recent book that gives the lie to the alleged decline of the family, it is this one.

Chapter 3

RELIGIOUS UNORTHODOXY

The Forgotten Topic: Religion

A MAJOR source of intergenerational conflict is religion—the senior generation being strongly fixed by and large in old religious ways and loyalties; the middle and young generations tending to be more tolerant or more ecumenical, as the case may be, about deviations from familial religious traditions. Take the Greens and the Fitzgibbons down my street. They settled the problem of a mixed marriage between a Lutheran daughter and a Catholic son by the marriage taking place in a Congregational church. On the surface this may have seemed reasonable to the neighbors, but it created all sorts of problems within the respective families. Grandparents on both sides were disapproving of the arrangement and wondered whether they should attend the ceremony. One grandparent felt obliged to exert pressure on behalf of her particular church. This created tension between the three generations of the Fitzgibbons family, and it spilled over to involve the other family to the marriage. It was a grand mess.

The marriage went ahead as the young couple themselves wanted it. Which was as it should be. Unresolved, however, was the myriad issues raised by the intrusion of religious unorthodoxy into a family, a common occurrence these days given the social and religious reconstructions that have taken place in the country and in churches.

Curiously enough, religion is not a topic that particularly occupies professionals who work with the aged. Following a "You and Your Aging Parents Conference" at the Andrus Gerontology Center at the University of Southern California in May, 1978, Helen Dennis compiled a bibliography of more than a hundred references relating to intergenerational topics and issues from the articles, books and reports cited or presented by the conference's faculty. The subject of religion, she noted, was "conspicuously absent" from the list. Religion did not come up in the major conference presentations. It's a familiar story.

This section of the book does not pretend to answer all the questions that can arise involving the generations within a family when religious unorthodoxy upsets the tranquillity of old family customs, habits, and beliefs. But it does examine some common ones and, in so doing, may provide guidelines with respect to others.

To Go or Not To Go, That Is the Question

A few summers ago, the placidity of the home of friends was disturbed by the announcement of a son that he was marrying—not in his church, not in her church, not even in a justice's office, but rather in exotic improvised rites by the seashore at which the principals would be garlanded with flowers and the guests would be invited to tote balloons, carry daffodils, or bear some other article of gaiety and light. The announcement threw the senior generations into something of a religious and authoritarian dilemma. The authoritarian dilemma resolved itself soon enough, for after all the anguished and angry words were said, the senior generations had to face the inescapable: the son was an adult; his life was his own; he could do as he pleased. So could she.

That left the religious dilemma for the parents and the

grandparents to grapple with. Should they attend or not attend? To attend might seem to convey some sort of blessing on a ceremony which the elders in the family considered outlandish and religiously unorthodox. But not to attend would in effect be a rejection of the son and could result in an alienation that would be years in the correcting. Does one go or not go?

The answer, of course, is easy enough. The wonder is that so many people find it difficult to come to and afterwards lug around burdened consciences.

You attend the ceremony, naturally.

Michael A. Creedon of the Catholic University of America Center for the study of Preretirement and Aging put it this way: "You go to their balloon ceremony in the woods or on the beach, or whatever. We all want our children and our grandchildren to have our values, but that isn't the way of life. Every generation works out its own values. The challenge of the elderly in this regard is the challenge of diversity and of accepting social change and different lifestyles. It's the ability to accept others as they are." Creedon was not suggesting that parents and grandparents extend their blessing to everything the new generation adopts unto itself. One does not have to be joyous about everything they do, he commented. Indeed it would be ludicrous to pretend that one was. "You accept the person, not what the person is doing," Creedon added. "It's a variation in a way on Pope John XXIII's counsel with respect to Communists: Love them; reject the system." The point, he concluded, is "not to get sterilized, not to get fixed in one's ways and attitudes, but to be open to change. This is the stimulation of age."

A nun-friend of mine faced something of the same dilemma when her Catholic nephew elected to marry in a

Baptist church. The whole family looked to her lead: parents, grandparents, aunts, uncles, cousins.

"I went," she said. "Everyone in the family was watching what I would do, and what I did would determine the mind of others. If I stayed away, many others would have. This would have been a disaster. It would have increased distress, solidified resentments, and split my nephew off from people who love him very much—and whom he loves dearly. I went, and it made such a difference to everyone. I made a decision based on family.

"Yet it could just as easily have been a decision based on theology," she added in specific Catholic context. "The Catholic Church is in such a flux these days that many young people have known only a church that is changing, and naturally they wonder, is the church that changed from fish on Friday, the Latin of the Mass, and so much else, going to change on the where and the wherefore of a marriage ceremony? I can understand that.

"I can also be sympathetic to my nephew's point that marriage is no less a sacrament because it is taking place in a Protestant instead of a Catholic church. After all, couples do marry themselves. The priest or minister or rabbi is merely the official witness.

"But, as I said, that's not what dictated my decision to go to my nephew's marriage. I went out of love, and because I thought it more important to demonstrate that love than to stick by some rule which might alienate him entirely—from members of the family and his own faith."

Though my nun-friend rationalized out of a definite religious denominational context, the conclusion at which she arrived was enlightened in the best ecumenical sense. Indeed hers is a rationale that can be applied across the Judaeo-Christian spectrum. Love should be the dominating and determining factor when religious issues bring the generations of a family into conflict, and wise are the parents, adult children, and aged grandparents who remind one another of this.

When Grandparents Play Priest

It's an old story nowadays. There is a new grandchild in the family, but months pass and the parents do nothing about the child's religious initiation. This can be disturbing in Christian families, and most particularly in Catholic ones, where the tradition is that a new baby is baptized within a few weeks and at most a few months of birth. Today it is not uncommon for parents to have no plans for such a ceremony. The reasons range from indifference, to casualness, to outright loss of belief. What are the grandparents' responsibilities in instances of these sort? Should they steal the baby away and have it secretly baptized, a practice not unknown in the past? Or should they baptize the baby themselves, as missionary nurses are reported to have done wholesale in so-called pagan lands to say nothing of some hospital nurses in certain metropolitan cities?

It is a delicate issue, concedes Paulist gerontologist Edward J. Gorry of Los Angeles, "not only because of the church doctrine and pastoral practice involved, but also because the answer can be a source of offense to well-meaning Christian grandparents, who honestly believe that they are conscience-bound to intervene and take action."

That is not their role!

Gorry explains: "The 'privileges' of grandparenting are not to be identified with the role and responsibility of being a godparent. We must uphold the natural rights of the parents, understand the acquired spiritual rights and responsibilities of the designated godparents, and not

liberally indulge the customary prerogative of grandparents always to know how a child ought to be raised (and
frequently spoiled).

"Add to that a clearer understanding of the official
church teaching on the subject of baptism, and we have the
mixings of some guidelines and criteria to handle infant
baptism without resorting to the Archie Bunker procedure
of sneaking the child away from the parents and offering it
for 'christening' at a parish where a kindly old monsignor
loves to ransom pagan babies.

"In the ceremony of baptism, the priest asks the following question of the parents and godparents: 'You have
asked to have your child baptized. In doing so you are accepting the responsibility of training this child in the practice of the faith. It will be your duty to bring this child up
to keep God's Commandments as Christ taught us, by loving God and neighbor. Do you clearly understand what
you are undertaking?' The godparents serve as official rep-
resentatives of the community of faith and, with the parents, actively request baptism for the child. After the baptism, the godparents are to serve as proxies for the parents
if the parents are unable or fail to provide for the religious
training of the child. They may prudently have to intervene
if occasion requires in order to carry out their responsibility."

Inevitably the next question is, "Do grandparents have
an equal right and responsibility to intervene?"

"No, they do not," responds Gorry.

Should they be concerned?

"Yes, says Gorry, "if they truly love their child, his or
her spouse, and the grandchild. But their area of activity
should lie more in attempts to influence and persuade than
in trying to assert a right to take over. They do not or-

dinarily have that right if the parents are still in charge and the child is under the jurisdiction of those parents.''

In other words, hands off! The child belongs to the parents, not the grandparents, and the decision to be made, or in the case of baptism not made, is theirs. It is true in Catholicism. It is true in all religions.

Must the grandparents forever, then, stand aside on questions relating to the spiritual or religious formation of the child? Gorry's answer is sagacious:

''As the child grows out of infancy, the opportunity for the grandparents to contribute to the spiritual welfare of the child increases according to the ability they have to influence the child without alienating the child and the child's parents. Tact, prudence, and love are the factors brought into play here. Now a grandparent may begin to look like a godparent to the child without looking like an intruder to the parents. But even here we have to remember St. Paul's caution that even if a thing is lawful, it is not always necessarily expedient.''

Divorce Comes to the Family

Aline Coghlan is a pastoral counselor at St. John the Baptist parish in Silver Spring, Maryland. She told newspaper interviewer Katharine Bird that when she first started on the job her services were sought mostly by couples having trouble with their children. In five years, she said in 1982, all that has changed. Now most of those who come to her come with marital problems. It's a husband or wife saying, ''I can't take it any more.''

Her experience is not surprising. The breakdown of marriages, especially among couples in their 40s and 50s, an age group Coghlan finds very vulnerable, is at near epidemic proportions. In the ten years between 1970 and

1980, divorces increased nationally from 3.5 to 5.3 per 1,000 population. In 1978 there were 1,130,000 divorces in the country; in 1979, 1,181,000 divorces, and in 1980, 1,195,000. The median duration of marriages is now only 6.5 to 6.8 years. Pretty sobering figures.

All kinds of factors figure into divorces, and one of the most serious is one that never appears in the run-down of causes: delay. People whose marriages are in trouble delay before seeking help. They wait until a severe breakdown has occurred in the marital relationship, and it is just too late. Coghlan finds that she is seldom able to help couples who delay to mend their relationship.

The advice is obvious: The wise person with a physical complaint does not dally in seeking medical help; similarly, the wise couple with marital problems should not dally in seeking marital counseling.

The subject of divorce comes up here because divorce is generally thought of as affecting the principals and their children, whereas divorce also has strong consequences *up* the generational ladder. One's aged parents can be as completely devastated by a divorce as the divorcing parties themselves and the children of the marriage, and they too must be thought of and prepared emotionally for the event.

Take Agnes and Tom, Catholics. They belong to a family line to which divorce was completely foreign. Oh, a cousin disappeared once, going off to Florida to start a new life. But he was not skipping town on a wife. He was ducking out on a girl whom he had gotten pregnant. If you were a Catholic, that was much less a scandal in the old days than getting a divorce. Indeed, it was almost a form of high-jinks, God save the mark. Anyway, divorce arrived in Agnes' and Tom's family when a son announced that he and his wife were splitting. There were three children. Agnes and Tom were inconsolable, and went on a guilt trip of their own. Where had they failed? What should they have done differently? Had they not acted when they should have?

Questions such as these are meaningless and irrelevant, and to pursue them accomplishes nothing of value. Rather, it could aggravate one's own physical and emotional equilibrium. The divorce belongs to the principals to the action, and any others are foolish to burden themselves unnecessarily with the whys and wherefores. This does not mean that one's parents should be completely detached from the divorce action of a son or daughter. But it should be made clear to them that they should not take upon their shoulders a weight that properly belongs to others. The dutiful son or daughter will help understandably anxious parents to appreciate that fact.

Father Joseph M. Hayden of Bridgeton, New Jersey, has suggested, in *CGA World,* some useful guidelines for senior parents when a son or daughter divorces:

Examine your own feelings. "Are you sorry for your child—or for yourself? If the breakup seems a disgrace to the family name, if what others will think is uppermost in your mind, then you, not your adult child, are the center of your concern. Feeling sorry for the wrong person (yourself) only chokes your relationship with your offspring."

Get rid of guilt. "Trying to find ways to blame yourself for the failure of your child's marriage is, in almost every case, a futile and unnecessary waste of time."

Don't say "I told you so"—even if you did. "Wounded partners in a dissolving marriage don't need any snipers on the sidelines. Maybe your son or daughter should have known better, but what's needed now is your friendship and understanding."

Decide which "line" to take. "Some may take what seems to be the soft line and say, 'The door of your old home is always open.' Others may take a tough stance and declare, 'When you left home you started your own independent life. You'll just have to work things out for yourself.' Only you can figure out which response is the right one for you, but it is important to work this through in your own heart, on the basis of what you can handle, and not because of appearance alone. . . . Sincerity is vital."

Be careful about giving advice. "This is the most dangerous territory of all, for what might be healing medicine for one couple could be poison for another. Each marriage, like the partners in it, is unique, and there are not bromides that work for all. You may actually complicate matters by offering too much advice, particularly if the couple are already receiving professional counseling."

Never withdraw your moral support. "Hurt people need healing, not a judicial chamber. Parents are called upon to provide the best kind of unconditional love they can muster. This may be difficult to do, but by ridding yourself of self-centeredness, personal guilt, and the desire to control your grown child's life and decisions, you can be free to provide genuine love and caring."

Retirement Can Rock a Marriage

If there is a flip side of the divorce-in-middle-age disc, it is the tension-late-in-life tune. Retirement can test the happiest of marriages.

The Spauldings had a happy—indeed, almost blissful marriage. They had moved around a lot in connection with

Jim Spaulding's work, finally settling in New York City where Jim served as an executive officer in a publishing house. At 65, Jim retired, and he and his wife Rita went off to the coast of Maine to count sea gulls, enjoy lobster, and live the good life of the retirement years. Or so they thought. They were no sooner settled down in Maine than Jim was dreadfully unhappy. He and his wife bickered; the bickerings graduated to heavy arguments; before you knew it, they were talking of separation and divorce. Their children were astonished and wondered what had happened to Mom's and Dad's happy marriage. Mom wondered what had happened to the husband she thought she knew inside and out after almost 40 years of marriage.

For his part, Jim put the blame on Maine, but later, as he looked back on the experience as a retirement survivor, he realized the causes were himself and the psychological traumata that so often accompany retirement.

Can retirement put a strain on marriage?

"It most certainly can," says the Reverend Robert E. Fillinger, a specialist in gerontological studies at Gordon-Conwell Theological Seminary in South Hamilton, Massachusetts, and particularly in instances where the retiree is a man and the wife has stayed home most of the years of the marriage.

"A man can't take care of his rose garden eight hours a day," remarks Fillinger. "He's done by noon. 'Now what do I do with my time?' he asks himself. If there's no good answer to that question, then a strain very well could develop. It's easy enough to understand. More than likely the man found much if not all of his meaning and significance in a job. Now he doesn't have a job any more, and he has little to do with his time. He's in a new world physically and psychologically. It's different for the woman.

She still has her household chores to occupy her, the meals to prepare, and very likely her clubs and church groups to get out to. For her nothing has changed, except *he's* around all day. *He's* unhappy and restless, and she has a presence in the house that wasn't there before, at least not constantly. You know the old saw, 'I married you for better or for worse, but not for lunch.' Well, there you have it. Strains do set in while adjustments are made. For both partners.''

These were not exactly the complications in the Spauldings' case. Jim Spaulding suffered the common and often personally unsensed effects of retirement: loss of role, loss of status, loss of purpose by being no longer productive, and finally loss of self-respect. Rita Spaulding suffered loss of privacy (the house had been hers all day long after the children left), loss of kitchen management (she could not even make a salad any more without coaching), and was threatened with a loss of independence as Jim crowded her every moment. Pick up a phone to call Mildred, and he would have half an ear cocked.

The Spauldings worked out of their difficulties themselves. He got a small job as a proofreader that took him out of the house for a few hours every day—just enough to restore the distance in everyday relationships that most people need to be more interesting to one another. Now there were things to talk about again in the evening. Jim's self-esteem eased its way back, thanks to his "second-career" job. Before he knew it, he was loving retirement.

The Spauldings were lucky. Their marriage endured the strain of retirement. They did not even have to see a marriage counselor, although early in their time of strain it would have been most helpful to them if they had. Their mistake—one that all adult children should beware in terms of themselves as well as with respect to their parents—is that they walked into retirement blind. "Walk into retirement blind," comments Fillinger, "and you're going to bump hard into problems of idleness, loss of status, confusion about one's worth, and the meaning of life itself. All can rock a marriage mightily."

So what is the solution?

One solution, according to Fillinger, is preretirement education. A few corporations have preretirement educational programs for their executives, and some unions are thinking about such a program for their members. But only thinking. For most people in society, there is nothing by way of organized program to prepare for retirement. Nothing, that is, except the individual or the individual's family—and what the sensible person, the sensible family can do to insure that retirement is not a traumatic test of one's marriage or one's ability to adjust and cope. Dr. Fillinger's advice: Just don't wait until it is too late.

"There's probably no ideal age at which to start thinking and preparing for retirement," says Dr. Fillinger, "although I suggest no later than 55, and probably before then. Certainly financial preparation should begin no later than 55, and even then it is probably too late because there is not enough time to accumulate a sufficient reserve to supplement one's Social Security. But at 55 it isn't too late to act in other areas. At 55 one can begin tooling up for a second career, and, just as important, one can begin reading up on the experience of retirement so as to be aware of some of the psychological aspects of that state in life. One can also begin to experiment with the productive uses of leisure time, and be alert to diet and health maintenance. There is much that one can do for oneself, so that when one is actually retired one can understand what is happening and appreciate that it is not all bad. Retirement can be an exciting, pleasant, productive time. But one must be prepared for it."

The wise adult child can help parents of retirement age move gracefully into this new stage in life by adopting Fillinger's counsel. Get the parents thinking early about retirement, taking special care to insure that they understand that retirement involves adjustments which can be difficult and painful. Check out the literature on retirement and place the best and most appropriate of it in the parents' hands. Finally, encourage the retiring parents to use their time constructively. Retirement should not be wasted just hanging around and watching television. Look into continuing education programs at the local high schools, at area colleges, at Elderhostels, and encourage the retiring parent especially to consider taking courses or classes that will enrich what could otherwise be barren intellectual or occupational years. (More on this subject in the "Continuing Education" section of chapter 10.)

Chapter 4

KEEPING FIT

Overseeing the Aged Parent's Health

IT is a truism, of course: everyone is responsible for his or her own health. But there comes a time in many families when this responsibility passes beyond the individual and involves others. This is particularly so, for instance, in cases of aged persons who suffer confusion or otherwise have difficulty in coping with life's problems. Then a son or daughter must be prepared to be assertive, to be ready to step in and ask, "What is this medication? On whose directions are you taking it? What is it for? Are you taking it as prescribed, as with food, or orange juice, or plenty of water? Is there anything to be avoided while one is taking this medicine, like alcohol?" It might be a good thing to check back with the doctor on the person's answers.

According to Peter P. Lamy, head of the Department of Pharmacy Practice and Administrative Science at the University of Maryland School of Pharmacy in Baltimore, an especially important time to check on a person's medication is towards the end of a hospital stay. "Hospital discharge is a peak time of medication change," declares Lamy. "The patient may have been taking six or eight drugs when admitted, and these prescriptions are likely to be changed. Upon discharge, there may be six or eight new medications. It should be clear whether or not the old drugs are to be continued. The patient may have learned slowly the proper way to take the former drugs. Several new ones all of a sudden can be highly confusing.''

Further, it is important to know what side-effects to expect from a medicine. A pill for hypertension might cause mild depression. Another might raise havoc with the sinuses. I know a person who rushed around for years turning off air conditioners and feeding himself with antihistamines because he thought he had a perpetual head cold. The ''head cold'' turned out to be his reaction to reserpine, a high blood pressure medication. ''If the patient understands what to expect from a drug, then he or she can report back whether the drug is doing what it was intended to do and whether unexpected side effects have developed,'' Lamy comments. ''With that information, the doctor can determine the drug's efficacy, or whether the dose or the medication itself needs to be changed.'' The children of aged parents should not let the old folks be the sole custodians of this information.

Some other points on which to be alert:

Sleeping pills. Be on guard against one's aged parents becoming reliant on sleeping pills. People over 60 constitute only 15 percent of the population, but they consume 40 percent of the sleeping pills taken in this country! Further, because of age and the probability that they are already on medication of some kind, older persons are considered to be at more risk from the harmful side effects of sleeping pills. For one thing, older persons are constitutionally slower in breaking down and excreting the drugs in sleeping pills, and this could result in daytime drowsiness and impaired alertness. There is also the possibility of toxic reaction when sleeping pills are indiscriminately combined with one's regular medication. As for those benign advertisements for sleeping pills that one constantly encounters on television, be wary. As *Modern Maturity* has pointed out, the general body of knowledge about the safety of sedative/hypnotic drugs is largely derived from studies of younger adults, and the results do not necessarily apply to older persons. The wisest course for anyone having trouble sleeping is to consult with a doctor.

Hot weather. Keep a warm-weather watch on the old folks. The elderly do not adjust nearly as well as younger persons to increases in temperatures, partially because they perspire less. And once again medications may be a complicating factor, as they may decrease resistance to heat stress. So may an underlying disease. Consequently, during times of high temperature and high humidity, the elderly are advised to be cautious, the more so if they have problems such as heart disease, a stroke, or diabetes. An inordinate build-up of body heat can result in heat stroke or heat exhaustion.

Heat stroke is the failure of all body cooling mechanisms and is marked by faintness, dizziness, headache, nausea, loss of consciousness, rapid pulse, flushed skin, and high body temperature (104 F/40 C). Heat stroke is a medical emergency requiring immediate medical attention and care by a doctor.

Heat exhaustion is a more common form of hot-weather illness. It takes longer to develop, and results from loss of bodily fluids and salt. Its symptoms are weakness, heavy sweating, nausea, and lightheadedness. Heat exhaustion is relieved by rest in a cool place and the restoration of body water through drinking cool fluids. Sponge baths and the application of wet towels to the face and body will also help in lowering body temperatures.

Hot weather can also bring on heat syncope, marked by dizziness, fatigue, and sudden faintness, and heat cramps, which could involve pains to the abdomen, arms, or legs. Both conditions are eased by rest, cooling off, and the taking of extra fluids. If it is necessary to replace the salt in the body lost in heat attacks, this should be done only under a doctor's supervision.

Cold weather. Hypothermia is the medical word for the condition associated with an abnormally low internal body temperature. Hypothermia is a killer, although how much of a killer is not precisely known. Accurate data is lacking, partly because its symptoms are like those of many other illnesses. However, figures collected in Great Britain over the past 25 years suggest that about 10 percent of persons over age 65 are at risk.

This much is certain: A person is especially vulnerable to hypothermia if he or she. . . .

• Lives alone or is isolated, without a phone to reach help in case of accident or illness;

• Does not shiver or react normally to cold;

• Is ill or unable to move around well;

• Is taking drugs that keep the body from regulating temperature normally. Such drugs include phenothiazines, which are commonly used to treat anxiety, depression, nausea, and other conditions.

Also at risk are the chronically ill, the very old, those unable to afford enough heat, and those who do not take the normal steps to keep warm. I know a woman in her 80s, who insists that she is never cold and who will take long walks on cold winter days wearing no stockings at all. She is flirting with hypothermia; indeed she courts it.

That woman is not wise, for even mildly cool temperatures can trigger hypothermia—temperatures, for instance, in the 60–65 F (15.5–18.3 C) range for those incapable of generating sufficient body heat. Also, hypothermia can be contracted without the elderly person even sensing it, since that individual does not respond to cold in the same way as a younger person—or in the same way that very individual reacted to cold when he or she was of younger years.

How does one know when a person is suffering from hypothermia? According to the National Institute of Health, it is when the individual's temperature is below 95 F (35 C) or does not register on an oral thermometer. (A rectal thermometer is recommended for a more accurate reading.) Emergency medical help is needed instantly. Other symptoms: a change in appearance or behavior during cold weather; uncontrollable shivering, lack of shivering, or stiff muscles; low indoor temperatures, and other signs that the person has been in an unusually cold room; slow and sometimes irregular heartbeat, slurred speech, shallow and very slow breathing; weak pulse; low blood pressure; confusion, disorientation, or drowsiness; or having lapsed into a coma, which is very probable when the body temperature drops to 90 F (32.2 C) or under.

How can the elderly be protected against hypothermia? By keeping living and sleeping areas heated to 65 F (18.3 C), although it should be noted that people who are sick may need higher indoor temperatures; and by dressing warmly during the day, eating enough food, and staying as active as possible. Because hypothermia may start during sleep, special care should be taken about wearing enough clothing and using enough blankets.

Older persons on medication for anxiety, depression, nervousness, or nausea should check with their doctor about the possible effects of their medications on bodily temperature.

Finally, older persons should be careful about being alone for too long a period of time, particularly in times of severe cold.

The Importance of a Correct Diet

There is probably no Bible story better known than the miracle of the loaves and the fishes. It involves the incident at Bethsaida-Julias, where Jesus is reported to have fed a throng of 5,000 persons with two fishes and five loaves of bread that someone had in a single basket. The crowd ate its fill, and the remnants of the meal, when collected, multiplied into twelve baskets of left-overs. This story is told in the Bible to dramatize the powers of Jesus, but I argue that there is a subtle, secondary point overlooked by biblical exegetes. Note what Jesus fed the crowd. Not fatty beef. Not greasy lamb. Not sausage or salami. He fed them loaves and fishes. He knew what was good for them. The fish was not fried, and the bread was likely more crusty than doughy.

Diet is important to people of all ages, and the middle generation, thanks to dietetic discoveries of recent years, is generally alert to certain fundamental rules, such as watching starches and avoiding fats and salt. This is not so true of the older generation whose eating habits were formed when fats were considered a tasty adjunct to the meat and when you went easy, not on salt, but on pepper because it might give you an ulcer. It is hard to break old eating habits. I know an 80-year-old woman who persists in making a vegetable soup with a bouillon-cube base that is so salty it can float a silver spoon. Almost.

The National Institute on Aging in Bethesda, Maryland, has published a booklet on nutrition and aging which offers valuable dietary tips for everyone who is beginning to put on years. Persons with aged parents should be aware of it and of dietary guidelines generally, for they have a responsibility for their parents' well-being, and this extends to diet as surely as anything else.

A starting point is watching the older person's weight. Most people gain weight more easily as they grow older, but they need the same amounts of most nutrients (vitamins, minerals, and protein) as younger persons. This means that older people in particular should eat nutritious food and cut down on sweets, salty snack foods, high-calorie drinks, and alcohol.

Exercise is also important in keeping off extra pounds. A person who is exercising regularly can eat more without gaining weight than a person who sits most of the day.

Eating too little can be as harmful as eating too much. People who do not eat enough have less energy; they may become lonely and depressed. In addition, a diet containing too few calories is likely to be lacking in vitamins and minerals.

A well-balanced diet is one that provides adequate vitamins, minerals, protein, and carbohydrates. Such a diet is rich in fresh vegetables (especially leafy greens like kale, collard, turnip, and mustard greens), fresh fruits, low-fat dairy products, beans or meat, fish, and whole grains. Whole grain foods include whole-grain breads and cereals, oatmeal, whole wheat or rye crackers, barley, brown rice, and cornmeal. Eating these kinds of food will help reduce the amount of fat and salt in the diet. We all know, I hope, that too much fat and salt may contribute to heart disease, high blood pressure, and stroke.

One special piece of advice: People should talk with their doctors about their eating habits, or those of their parents, especially if illnesses are involved that might re-

quire changes in what or how much they eat. This is important because some medicines can interact with certain
foods and change the effects of the medications, and other
drugs can alter nutritional needs.

Exercising Under Doctors' Directions

For ten years or so, Americans have been on a fitness
kick, so that now nearly 70 million Americans engage regularly in some form of physical exercise. Next week some
20 million joggers will be on the streets, and another 6
million will be engaging in aerobic dancing. In fact, the
number of persons staying fit or working their way to fitness through some form of exercise program has doubled
in the last 20 years. Still, we are essentially a sedentary peo-.
ple, for millions of Americans do no exercise at all and 68
percent of those who start programs of regular exercise
quit by the end of 30 days. A recent Louis Harris poll in-
dicated that only 37 percent of Americans are faithful
about regular exercise, and among those over age 50, the
figure is down to 30 percent. This is very foolish, for exercise is important for everyone, and for the elderly no less
than a 40-year-old school teacher fighting a beer belly.

This is not a pitch to the adult child to rush out and buy
Grandma a jogging suit for Mother's Day, and Grandpa
some running shoes for his birthday. Overly strenuous exercise carries serious risks. You could end up picking them
up from alongside the road some day. But it is a pitch to
get one's older parents exercising, if not in some supervised
exercise program, then at least on their own, and preferably under the direction of their doctor. Even short walks
are good exercise for the elderly, which is why it might be
better for Grandma and Grandpa to get out and purchase
the daily paper at the corner store, rather than having it

dropped off on the doorstep. A two-block walk is better than no walk at all, although only marginally so. To be effective, exercise must be prolonged, frequent, and vigorous enough to increase significantly one's heart rate. Activity which meets these criteria is called aerobic conditioning. It challenges the heart and lungs to demand more oxygen and gradually builds up one's aerobic capacity— the ability to increase the delivery of oxygen-enriched blood to the body. The heart muscle is strengthened, and the blood vessels become more elastic, thus permitting a better blood flow.

There are solid reasons for encouraging exercise among the elderly. Studies have shown that people who stay active and exercise are more satisfied with life, and less prone to somatic, anxiety, and depressive symptoms. The studies are not to be sneered at.

Dr. James A. Blumenthal and Dr. R. Sanders Williams of the Duke University Medical Center have done extensive research in the area of exercise and aging, and have concluded that "a program of regular exercise throughout the life-span will reduce the prevalence of chronic illness and disability in older Americans and, further, will help foster improvement of their self-esteem, efficiency, and productivity."

Drs. Blumenthal and Williams conclude too that exercise helps prevent coronary disease by promoting cardiovascular fitness, which means greater stamina from a stronger heart and circulatory system. (More than 600,000 Americans die each year from heart disease.) Exercise, they say, is beneficial as well for several other specific medical problems that occur more frequently with advancing age. For example, mild exercise in people who are diabetics helps their cells make better use of insulin, the sugar-controlling hormone that they lack. But perhaps the most startling finding is the improved psychological condition among those who exercise regularly.

Blumenthal and Williams studied 16 older men and women in the course of a ten-week exercise program, and a matched control group of adults who simply maintained their sedentary lifestyles. All persons completed a battery of psychological tests, including measures of mood and personality function. Examination of test scores after the ten-week program revealed that the scores for the adults who exercised regularly improved, while the scores for the control group remained the same. Those in the exercise program scored lower on measures of anxiety, tension, depression, confusion, and fatigue, and scored higher on the vigor sub-scale than did the control group. The findings were reported in *Advances in Research,* the journal of the Duke University Center for the Study of Aging and Human Development.

The exercise program for the elderly of Drs. Blumenthal and Williams emphasizes such activities as stationary bicycling, stair climbing, swimming, and pool walking (wading in shallow water), rather than jogging—since inevitably there is increased risk of musculoskeletal injury for the elderly during exercise. Supervised exercise programs and use of proper equipment are encouraged as means of minimizing risks.

Exercise programs should not be indiscriminately thrust on elderly parents by their children. Much less should they be devised by the elderly themselves. They should prescribed by the elderly person's doctor, who will know what is best in the light of that person's medical history. But once the doctor prescribes, the recommendations should not be whimsically disregarded. Exercise is as important as medicine and should be taken as conscientiously as that diuretic pill or any other medicine the doctor prescribes. The adult child should see that the elderly parent is not careless about this. Exercise lowers blood pressure, reduces bodily weight, lessens the heart rate at rest and during exercise. As a dividend, exercise provides a mental boost, which often furnishes people an important incentive to stay active.

Keeping in Communication

It happened in my town last winter, but it is an old story and almost anyone can recite versions of it from one's own community experience: An elderly woman (although only 67, which really is not all that old) was not seen for several days. A visiting public health nurse came by in the course of appointed rounds and, not receiving an answer to her knocks, notified police, who entered through a cellar window and found the woman on the floor of a second-story bedroom. She was conscious, but unable to move because of injuries sustained in a fall. The woman lived alone. The telephone was downstairs. She had lain there almost three days before help arrived.

This story had a happy ending. The woman was transported in serious condition to Addison Gilbert Hospital in Gloucester, where she made her recovery. She is back now in her home out on the tip of Cape Ann, lucky to be alive, but no doubt subconsciously concerned that what happened once might repeat itself, next time with consequences that would be fatal.

It is a real concern to be sure. Yet chances of an incident of that sort happening can be lessened dramatically by a simple expedient: communication. Individuals who live alone—and this includes aged couples as well as single per-

sons, like the woman of my story—should make provision
to be in regular contact, preferably daily, with a son, a
daughter, a neighbor, a friend nearby, a distant relative—
anyone, just so that unpleasant eventualities are covered in
instances of emergency. A son might phone; a daughter-in-
law might pop in while out shopping or running the car
pool; a neighbor might be alerted to watch that lights go on
and off consistent with habit, that the mail is collected,
that the newspaper is picked up. There are any number of
small, effortless steps which can be taken to insure that
Grandpa or Grandma, or cousin Nettie, is functioning to
form.

Chapter 5

BEING OLD AND SAFE

The Elderly Person As Crime Victim

IT was a pathetic story reported in the *New York Times*.

An 89-year-old woman sat in a wheelchair next to the witness stand in State Superior Court in lower Manhattan. She was the prosecution's witness in a case against her attorney, who was charged with stealing $129,000 from her and using the money for such things as a Cadillac, certificates of deposit listed in his and his wife's name, and real estate investments, also listed in his wife's name. The victim, a widow who lived alone and had no family, had contacted the lawyer and asked him to take care of her monthly expenses—"rent and gas and electric," small items such as those. She gave the lawyer her bankbooks, and records showed that he withdrew $72,000 almost immediately from one account, and the next day $57,000 from another.

The defendant's defense was not impressive. He claimed that the woman wanted "a greater yield" than she was receiving on her savings accounts, and accordingly he had made investments for her. He said further that his client had lent him money for the Cadillac and other items and that he had given her promissory notes but neglected to keep copies for himself.

It seemed an open and shut case, but here was the woman pleading with the judge and with her defense attorney to let her go home. "I was never in a mix-up like

69

this in my life," she remarked. "I feel as though I am just sitting here being persecuted for nothing, absolutely nothing."

The plea was understandable. The woman had been subjected over a period of days to a battering and often humiliating cross-examination that called into question her competence and her memory, the obvious purpose of which was to upset and confuse her and suggest to judge and jury that the defendant, not the old woman was the victim of an injustice. The tactic succeeded, for after deliberating several days the jury deadlocked. The vote was 11 to 1 in favor of conviction, but that one vote meant that the judge had to declare a mistrial and set a date for new proceedings.

The outcome, if one is allowed a judgment based on the thrust of the *Times'* account, dismayed police and prosecutors and quickened their concern about the physical and psychological barriers that prevent elderly victims of crime from becoming witnesses—which, in turn, makes it increasingly difficult to prosecute those who prey upon them. The problem is an old one, of course, but it is one that is becoming especially acute in times when age is less and less a protection against victimization.

There are no overall figures on crime against the elderly, but in New York City alone in 1982, the Police Department's seven senior-citizen robbery units investigated a total of 8,459 reported robberies. That seems an astonishingly large figure, yet it is only a fraction of the number of such robberies committed. For a number of reasons—fear, shame, failing eyesight, which makes it difficult to identify the attacker—many crimes against the elderly go unreported, unpursued, and therefore unprosecuted.

There is no sure-proof guard against victimization, but

adult children are doing their aged parents a distinct service when they caution them against dangers that lurk in
the society. To be cautious is not to be alarmist. The fact is
that the older generation grew up in a more innocent and
trusting time—a time when one could go out and leave
one's door unlocked; a time when one did not need double
and triple padlocks on the front and back doors, or bars on
windows. That time has largely gone, at least in most areas
of the country. It is important that older persons appreciate the realities of the new times, and it is not to be forever crying wolf to warn them that there are those out there
who would prey on them.

Must One Move to the Country To Be Safe?

Between 1975 and 1980, one million persons 55 or older
moved from urban to rural areas, while less than half the
number moved the other way. In 1980, 6.5-million persons
65 or over lived in rural areas, up from 5.4-million 10 years
before. The rural elderly population thus grew during the
1970s by 2.5 percent a year, twice its growth in metropolitan areas. The *Wall Street Journal* noted these figures
recently and attributed the trend to factors ranging on the
one side to the neighborliness, tranquility, and lower costs
in rural areas, and on the other to high costs, crowds, and
crime in urban areas. It was the crime factor that arrested
attention.

It is no secret that older persons suffer inordinately from
crime. There just aren't many Boy Scouts around helping
old men or women across streets these days. The unhappy
fact is that in many neighborhoods older persons today
risk being mugged, robbed, or beaten when they venture
alone on the streets. The teenager who helps the old
woman across the street may whip her purse away in the

process, which probably helps explain why, although about 80 percent of Americans live in metropolitan areas, only 68 percent of those 65 or older live there. In England, they have a quaint and telling term for those who prey on the elderly. They call them "Granny bashers."

The problem is that not everyone can pack up and move off to a safer rural or suburban area. And of course, not everyone would want to, which makes sense too. No one likes to be intimidated, and one of the most disagreeable forms of intimidation is that which works pressure on an individual to flee the old neighborhood. The issue then is safety. What precautions should be taken so that older persons will be more secure in their homes or apartments, and on the street when they venture outside? This is a question not only for the old folks, but also for adult children in their advisory role to their parents.

The Mayor's Commission on Affairs of the Elderly for the City of Boston has issued a booklet on the subject, "Safety Tips for You and Your Home." These are its recommendations:

At Home:

1. Always keep your doors locked with a good deadbolt lock. Don't depend on chain locks or doorknob latch locks.

2. Get window locks and use them. Ask your local police department what the best kind of window lock is.

3. Don't open your door to strangers—even if you have a chain on your door. Always ask for identification; this can be slipped under the door. If there's any doubt about someone, call the organization the person is from and ask if it has sent a representative to your home.

If you live in a high-rise building where you cannot see who is at the door before you buzz the person in, ask people who plan to visit to call you before they come. And know what time to expect your visitor.

4. Use your phone. Be sure it is in a place you can get to easily. Keep important numbers handy and near your phone.

5. Know and care about your neighbors. Watch out for them and they'll watch out for you. Keeping an eye on each other is not being nosy—it's being helpful.

6. Don't give information to strangers over the phone. Beware when a stranger asks for cash, talks about get-rich-quick schemes, tells you that you have to act fast, or that you'll get something for nothing. These are all ways the con man (or woman) will try to get something from *you* for nothing. (More on this in the next section.)

7. If you see anyone or anything suspicious, call the emergency police number, 911. Better to be safe than sorry.

8. Don't keep large sums of money or valuables in your home:

- The bank is the safest place for your money.
- Enroll in a Direct Deposit program at your bank.
- Have your Social Security checks sent directly to your bank.
- Pay your monthly bills by check.
- Keep your valuables—jewels, stocks, papers—in a safety deposit box.

9. When you leave your home—even if it is just for a short time—make it look occupied. Leave the TV or radio on, and during the night leave a light on.

10. If you're leaving for a day or more:

- Put your lights on an automatic timer, so they will go on and off by electric signal. You can also plug in a radio along with the lights.

• Let your friends and a neighbor know where and when you are going, and when you are expected back. Ask them to pick up things left outside your door, like advertising circulars, which could make your home look unoccupied.

11. Stop paper deliveries, and arrange for the Post Office to hold your mail.

(Boston has a program called Operation Ident-I-Guard, whereby individuals may have valuables marked through the Police Department. Individuals are then given Operation Ident-I-Guard decals for display in prominent places in the home. This is a good deterrent to potential burglars, for it announces to them that one's valuables have been marked with one's Social Security number and registered with the police. Individuals living in other cities or towns may wish to inquire if a comparable program is available in their community.)

On the Street:

1. Be alert and aware of your surroundings—don't daydream. Walk as though you know where you're going.

2. Always travel with a friend. If you are alone, travel in familiar territory.

3. Be cautious about talking to strangers. If someone approaches you, just keep walking. Sometimes it's proper not to be polite.

4. If you go out at night:
• Only go with a companion.
• Stay in familiar territory.
• Walk in well-lighted streets.
• Walk in the middle of the street. (If this is impossible, I would add, walk to the outer side of sidewalks, well away from doorways and alleys, where a potential attacker

could be lurking. A few steps' advantage is better than none.)

5. Do not leave your purse or briefcase unattended.

6. If you carry a purse, use a shoulder bag and keep it under your arm, close to your side, with the opening inside, next to your body.

7. Carry your keys separate from your purse or briefcase.

8. Don't carry large amounts of money. As already suggested:

• Enroll in Direct Deposit.

• Have your Social Security checks sent directly to your bank.

• Pay your monthly bills by check.

9. If you usually carry a hip wallet, don't. One's front pants pocket is a much safer place to carry money.

10. Always carry identification.

11. Carry a whistle; this can be used to call attention if one is in trouble.

12. When you take public transportation, always ride as close as possible to the driver.

Some additional safety tips:

• Be especially alert during the first days of the month, when Social Security, pension, public assistance, and other checks commonly arrive. This is a time when crimes against the elderly escalate, as the criminal knows it is when the elderly person is most likely to have money on hand.

• Consider a locked mailbox, as mailbox thefts are on the rise. For instance, nearly 20,000 Social Security checks are stolen each year, usually from mailboxes.

• Alarm systems are advisable, though they are expensive and not fool-proof. One of the best protections is a dog with a menacing or authoritative bark.

• See that there is proper illumination outside and inside one's house.

• Have some knowledge of self-defense and survival techniques.

• Use community escort services in localities where these are available.

It is, or course, regrettable that older people—indeed, all of us—live in an age when safety cannot be taken for granted, at least in terms of the yesterday most of us knew. Still, none of us should feel intimidated about moving about the community, and happily studies show that we are not, including the elderly among us. A survey of 4,000 elderly persons conducted by Pennsylvania State University confirms that the elderly are not inclined to confine themselves indoors because crime might befall them. One-third of the group said they were afraid in public parks, but they went anyway. Which is as it should be. No one should be reckless. On the other hand, no one should let hoodlums dictate the terms of his or her existence.

The Con-Artist Spares Not the Elderly

There is probably no one among us who has not read at one time or another about a confidence game, and then quietly patronized the victims with comments like, "The poor fools, what was the matter with them anyway?" Or, "They had it coming to them." It is the sort of comment that can come back to haunt, for we are all potential targets of the con-artist, and any one of us could be the victim of a con-game. It was only my own straitened circumstances that saved me once from being conned in Pittsburgh, when a bilker in an attempt to extort money persuaded me that he and I were college classmates. Later, in reflecting on the episode, I realized it was I who had proffered every piece of information which had seeded the notion, quite false, that maybe we indeed had been classmates.

There is a real pertinence in talking about con games in a book about adult children and aged parents, for con games are most often directed against older people. More's the pity, they succeed—not because the victims are greedy, anxious to make a quick buck, but generally because they have a desire to be helpful, friendly, and useful. So say police detectives who are experts on con games. Their word is reason to put the older persons in our lives on the alert against being victimized by the con artist, through their own naiveté and misplaced good intentions.

How common is the confidence game? Common enough for a giant organization like Citicorp, a New York-based international bank, to have included in a quarterly report a few years ago a warning captioned "Con Games Against Older People." According to Citicorp, the principal rip-offs are these:

• *The Pocketbook Drop.* On the street, a friendly, attractive young woman strikes up a conversation, says she is a widow and has just collected thousands of insurance dollars, which she shows you. Just then another woman comes up, looking perplexed. She has just found a purse and wonders what to do. She opens it. In a fat envelope inside is a large amount of cash and a suspicious letter. She says she'll go ask her boss, who is a lawyer, for his advice. She is his "secretary."

A few minutes later, she returns. Because of the suspicious letter, her boss thinks the money was lost by a gambler or someone hoarding money to avoid paying taxes. Her boss also thinks the three of you should share the money equally, but he wants to be sure you each have enough to live on for 60 to 90 days before it is legally safe to spend the found money.

He knows his secretary has her salary. The widow has her inheritance with her. The two women then suggest that you prove your financial responsibility by withdrawing a large sum from your bank. It sounds reasonable. You do so. All the cash is added to the envelope, and the secretary says she will bring it to her boss to hold. She returns a few minutes later and says her boss is counting the money and wants to see you. She gives you the address. Off you go to find the lawyer's office. It does not exist. Neither at this point does your money.

• *The Handkerchief Switch.* A bewildered young man approaches you on the street. He's a stranger in town, or a foreigner, or a visiting seaman looking for a hotel or rooming house. But since he can't read or write English, he can't find it. You say you'll help.

He pulls an envelope full of cash out of a large paper bag. He's willing to pay for your help. At that point another stranger comes by. He is shocked to see the first stranger carrying so much money. That, he says, should be in the bank. But the first stranger doesn't trust banks. How does he know that once he puts his money in the bank he can get it out?

The second stranger urges you to show him. He suggests that you withdraw a large sum from your own bank to prove how simple it is. The first stranger is overjoyed. He is so taken by your kindness that he asks you to hold his money for him for a few hours. He pulls out a nice, clean handkerchief, puts his money into it, says that for safety you should put your money in too. Then he ties everything into a neat bundle and shows you the safest way to carry it home. He gives you the money and says he will pick it up from you soon. The second stranger takes him to find his lodgings.

The owner doesn't return for his money soon, as he said he would. You get curious and open the bundle. There's been a switch. You're holding a handkerchief full of cut newspaper.

• *The Bank Examiner.* You get a call from a man who says he's a police officer or a bank examiner. Your help is needed. Some accounts at the bank, including yours, have been suffering unauthorized withdrawals. There may be a dishonest employee. Would you help trap the thief?

All you have to do is go to the bank and withdraw, in cash, the money in your account, leaving a few dollars in to keep the account open. He tells you to ignore any protests or questions by the teller. You'll be met back at home by a bank examiner or police officer who will hold your cash for you. A few days later your cash will be redeposited in your account.

You do it all—to help catch a thief. But when you check your account at the specified time, you discover there were no irregularities. The bank examiner or police officer wasn't genuine. Your money is gone.

There are other schemes, including variations of the above. New York City Police Department's Pickpocket and Confidence Squad, for instance, says that no day goes by without some bright, elderly person coming in to report that he or she has been the victim of the pocketbook drop.

Citicorp's advice for elderly persons: Be cautious. "Most people are honest. But there are still enough people—pleasant, friendly, convincing—who'll gladly take your last dollar and never stop smiling while they do it."

One other tip: Never give out the number of one's bank cash-checking or ID card to a telephone caller. There's a scheme whereby a pleasant voice calls and says your card has been found and will be left for you at the bank or police station. To verify that the card is yours, you are asked to tell the caller your personal identification code or number. You do and discover that your account has been tapped or cleaned out.

Thus, a basic piece of advice worth imparting to every older person: Steer wide of all sidewalk advances and double-check with another or others in the family all even slightly dubious propositions that involve money or property. Of course, it is possible that this other person or persons could be sucked into the con, but the chances are not great. Most con artists, and certainly the "small time" ones, tend to disappear into the landscape when their schemes broaden beyond intimate contact.

The elderly person is similarly advised to be on guard against fraud while around the house or familiar old haunts where one's guard is traditionally down. That winning, door-to-door salesperson or that friendly voice on the telephone has tricked many an older person into services that are not needed, insurance coverage that is useless, dancing lessons that are for the fatuous. The unscrupulous medicine man may seize the opportunity of an office call to foist unnecessary treatment on a person. The vast majority of doctors are honest persons, absolutely. However, it does not hurt to get a second opinion, particularly if one is dealing with someone new. It may save a lot of grief, and one's good health in the bargain. A woman across town from me underwent a questionably advised face lift not long ago. She was in her 80s. She died 10 days later of other causes. Had that unnecessary face lift triggered worry or strain, causing general collapse of the woman's health?

Why are the elderly so susceptible to fraud? According to Dr. Robert N. Butler in his book *Why Survive? Being Old in America* (New York, 1975), the reasons can be numerous: current medical status, the probability of organic brain damage, loneliness, grief and depression, fear of aging and death, pain and anxiety, educational level, personality, cultural characteristics, need. ("Why not chance it? I could use some extra bucks." That sort of thinking.)

Every age group is vulnerable to fraud, to be sure. But in the elderly the consequences are often so much more terrible—first, because the elderly have so much more to lose, perhaps their life savings; second, because the elderly person may be living on a fixed income, where even a small loss amounts to a severe deprivation; third, because there is less chance of the loss one day being made up, since the elderly person in all probability is not working.

So the prescription then is caution. Let the elderly person beware that there is someone out there with no compunctions about exploiting him or her. And let the adult child make sure that the elderly parent knows that fact of life.

Religious Cults and the Aged

Most of us think of religious cults in terms of our children, and the majority of us worry about children becoming caught up in them. Legitimately so, for cults can be, if not perverse, then much more than harmless things. Many indulge in deception and coercion. They are known to demand unquestioning loyalty to their authority figure. They are known to place insistence on the turning over of material possessions to the group. And they are known to exact strenuous physical labor of their members. To be sure, not all nonestablished religious movements fit this definition of cults; some nonestablished religious movements are in fact credited as authentic and accepted within the parameters of religious pluralism. But nowhere near all are authentic, and that is the difficulty. Many cults are exploitive and therefore dangerous.

The point here is that it is no longer just young people who are targets of religious cults, but older folks as well. For instance, both the Church Universal and Triumphant (CUT) and the Unification Church of the Korean evangelist Sun Myung Moon have made public declarations of intent to recruit from among the aged. One method is to gain access to retirement communities and homes for the aged, including nursing homes, as volunteers conducting meditation exercises, Bible study courses or entertainment programs, or as volunteers providing transportation and other services. Another method is to ring doorbells or work shopping malls and transportation depots. Whatever the method, the cults are often successful, particularly, it seems, in California and Florida, popular retirement states.

Why should older people be susceptible to religious cults?

Marcia R. Rudin, co-author with her husband James, of *Prison or Paradise, the New Religious Cults* (Philadelphia,

1980), cites such reasons as loss of belief in major societal institutions; substitution of utopian ideals for feelings of powerlessness to effect change through the political system; a desire for structure and order in a confusing world; and an increase in narcissism. According to Rudin in an interview in *Human Values and Aging Newsletter*, cults that emphasize abstinence, vegetarianism, and other physically oriented rites and regimens often satisfy the preoccupation with self that many people have.

The Archdiocese of Detroit's Department of Christian Service, has warned against religious cults in relation to the aged. Its newsletter *Response* carried the warning and identified as particularly vulnerable to the appeal of the cults the lonely and those feeling a need for companionship and direction. Cult members come along and provide "instant answers" to their problems, hold out the promise of a caring community, and, presto! have a new recruit. For many, the experience ends in disillusionment and a bilking. This is commonly accomplished by requiring the older person to turn over income from job or valuables, such as cash, jewelry, and property. Sometimes the recruit may be pressured into willing all he or she has to the cult. If the recruit is a working person, he or she may be acceptable while productive, then expelled from the cult without any financial resources when the older person becomes too old to work or becomes enfeebled.

Response is not spinning from whole cloth. Its information is supported by data from the Institute of Gerontology at Wayne State University in Detroit.

How does one protect against the intrusion of religious cults?

Response's recommendations are embraced in a series of

questions intended essentially for parish communities, but they are applicable to individuals in their own family situations:

- Do we leave the elderly of our family lonely, neglected, and alienated?
- Do we have homebound persons who are uncared for?
- Do we alienate an elderly individual who attempts to volunteer or otherwise assume acts of initiative?
- Are there hungry elderly who are related to us, or those without housing and proper medical attention?

The questions are slightly adapted here, for humanitarian concern is not an organized thing. It is each of us acting responsibly on our own to help others and most immediately those in our own family. If Mom or Dad joins a religious cult, it may be his or her constitutional right. But it may also be a huge mistake traceable to a son's or daughter's carelessness and neglect.

Chapter 6

SENIOR CRIME AND ALCOHOLISM

The Issue of Senior Crime

IN Brockton, Massachusetts, an 86-year-old man and his 63-year-old daughter were arrested not long ago on charges of selling marijuana, a business enterprise the two had taken up to supplement their Social Security income. The man received $338 a month from Social Security; the daughter, $404. There were weekly grocery bills, the daughter's 18-year-old son to support, and other expenses. "We weren't making a lot of money," said the woman of the marijuana enterprise, "just getting a little breathing room for the bills. We'd make $75 or $80 [a week] for the groceries." The father and daughter were innocents, in a way. They sold only to adults. If anyone looked marginal, they demanded to see an ID card proving that the person was at least an 18-year-old.

Other senior lawbreakers are not so naive. In January, 1982, the wire services carried a story on a 63-year-old woman who was picked up for luring "elderly and defenseless men" into her car with offers of rides, later drugging them with spiked drinks and robbing them. About the same time the CBS Sunday evening program "60 Minutes" was featuring a segment on senior shoplifters, who ostensibly were supplementing Social Security income by pocketing toothpastes, sun-tan lotions, cigarettes, and other minor essentials. Apparently an item stolen was a penny saved.

Stories such as these raised the specter of a new breed of lawbreaker, the once law-abiding person made aberrant in her or his older years by strained financial circumstances or other social factors. If adult children were prompted to ask themselves, "Hey, is Mom or Dad likely to become a crook?" it was no wonder. National newspaper, magazines, and television were all suggesting that older people were turning to crime in increasing numbers.

Actually such reports of a new criminal class proved to be vastly exaggerated. As organizations like the American Association of Retired Persons have reported, the number of older persons committing crimes has not grown significantly in the past decade and is not likely to in any foreseeable future. Suggestions about a new criminal class are nothing but a bad rap.

On the other hand, that some individuals in the senior generations are forced to steal to make ends meet should be a caution of sorts to adult children to check into the finances of their parents to make sure that they have income enough to meet expenses. This should be done delicately so as not to wound the parents' pride, and it should be done in all cases where it seems the parents may seem to be in marginal circumstances. Very frequently embarrassment or pride will deter parents from speaking out about their needs, so it is up to the adult children to take the initiative. Who knows? A precaution taken now may save a lot of embarrassment tomorrow.

The Problem of Senior Alcoholism

Senior crime may be something of a media myth, but arrests of seniors for alcohol-related offenses is not, and this is a problem that every adult child should be alert about. There has been enormous concern in recent years about high-school drinking and drinking on college campuses.

But older persons drink, too, many of them much more than they should. For instance, they drive while drinking, and they are arrested for it in numbers that are increasing in an alarming degree. In California, in 1980, of 31,390 arrests of older persons (2 percent of the total number of arrests that year in the state), nearly 69 percent were for driving under the influence or for other criminally drunk offenses. This amounted to 21,531 arrests!

Alcohol is a serious problem among older people, and not just in California. Indeed, alcoholism is listed first among the 25 most frequent diagnoses for Medicare inpatient treatment by the Health Care Financing Administration. The rating is based on a sampling of 20 percent of all Medicare inpatient hospital bills submitted to the HCFA for payment in 1977 and 1978.

According to the National Council on Alcoholism, senior citizens suffering from problem drinking comprise about 7 percent of the population. The figure is somewhat lower than that for the general population, because, as a rule, death decimates those with alcoholism problems much earlier in life through complications which deteriorate health. Alcoholism is actually the fourth leading killer in the United States, causing more than 85,000 deaths annually through such factors as liver diseases, automobile accidents, and crime. As for senior-citizen alcoholics, they may be either the "survivors" of a long history of drinking or so-called new cases. In any case, older people drink—to such an extent that there are those who maintain that the National Council on Alcoholism's estimates are much too low, that more like 10 percent of persons who are over 60 have a drinking problem.

What is known for sociological certainty is that the number of senior alcoholics is large, surprisingly larger than many have suspected in the past. One reason for this is that it is a problem that only lately has been looked at closely. For years it remained virtually hidden: partly because older people lead less visible lives, and partly because specialists in alcoholism prefer on the whole to treat younger persons, for whom rehabilitation means a return to employment or something more gainful than a life lived in retirement. What is generally agreed on is that alcoholism strikes hard at the bored, the lonely, and those burdened with losses of loved ones, or status, or purpose in life. This makes prime candidates out of older people.

This fact is borne out in a study on common aspects of senior alcoholism by sociologist Martha Knoy and reported in the journal *GeronTopics.*

Female alcoholism, according to her study, tended to be prevalent among the recently widowed and particularly among women who had few outside activities and had been moderate drinkers for years. Consumption of alcohol increased after the husband's death as the women relied on alcohol to ease the anxieties of long days and lonely nights.

Male alcoholics, Knoy discovered, often were men in a retirement crisis which resulted in inactivity and a fear of poverty. Unlike the woman—who, for the most part, were solitary drinkers—the men tended to drink with other men in bars or gathering places. They had been moderate to heavy drinkers for years. Now they drank more.

Another reason for increased drinking, a reason common both to women and men, was the use of alcohol as a form of self-medication for assorted untreated physical or emotional discomfits. Often, Knoy found, it grew out of the attitude, "So what—I have nothing to live for anyway."

Going beyond Knoy's study, alcoholism in older persons also derives from the relaxed atmosphere of retirement. Every week is a vacation week; every weekend a holiday weekend. With no demands of the work place impinging on one's time and fewer responsibilities at home (chances are the kids are grown and gone), the tendency is to relax more—to have the first drink at 4 o'clock instead of 5; to serve highballs instead of tea to the bridge-club group; to hang around longer in the clubhouse after a round of golf; to stiffen the content of that nightcap.

The Andrus Foundation of the AARP has awarded a research grant to the Institute of Gerontology at Wayne State University in Detroit to study the incidence of alcoholism among older persons. But one does not have to await the findings of that study to filter down to the grassroots for the individual to know what to do. The course of action is obvious: Get the problem drinker into Alcoholics Anonymous. If it is you, get yourself in; if it is your parent, get her or him in.

There is no disputing the effectiveness of A.A. as a program of moral and spiritual regeneration. A.A's 12 steps to sobriety have rescued many a life and saved many a family. The problem is that many persons are reluctant to give A.A. a try, usually because of feelings of false pride or shame. Of course a decision to enter A.A. takes courage. But making that decision may be all the difficulty there is in the process. I know a woman who battled with herself for years before she was able to work up the courage to attend her first A.A. meeting. She left bolstered by the experience—and amazed at how many old friends and neighbors she met there. It was like going to a block party, she said.

A Sickness, Not a Failing

Down in St. Charles, Virginia, deep in Appalachia, a nun who was once a high school principal in Stamford, Connecticut, works among the poor. She left a challenging post in a city that has taken on new life as a corporate headquarters community to initiate an apostolate in a place that is struggling and remote, among a people, many of whom cannot even read or write. Her name is Sister Beth Davies of the Congregation of Notre Dame, and hers is a true story.

I interviewed Sister Beth Davies in connection with my book *The New Nuns* (Fides/Claretian, 1982), locating her in Trenton, New Jersey, where she was assisting as an intern in a detoxification center and completing studies for certification as an alcoholism counselor. It seemed a curious place to find her, but she made things clear quickly and candidly.

"I'm here because I'm an alcoholic myself," she exclaimed. "I know a lot about the disease from personal experience, and I know the excellent treatment I was given. The poor deserve no less. It has been a real gift in my life to experience such powerlessness. Through it I am able to identify with the 'oppressed of the oppressed' in the mountains, who are cast aside as moral lepers. Through it I have come to know what it means to die in order to live. That's a gift. Gifts are given not to be kept for oneself; they're given to be shared. I want to share what I have learned, and whom I have come to be, with people who share the same disease."

That is a very beautiful commentary, and one of the details to note carefully is Sister Beth Davies' use of the word "disease" to categorize alcoholism.

Time was when alcoholism was regarded as a failing of character, an obnoxious self-indulgence. This was a terribly judgmental attitude, and families are warned to guard against resurrecting it.

Actually, the growing practice in some professional circles is to regard alcoholism as a triple sickness: one of the body, the mind, and the soul. Accordingly, a threefold approach to the problem has been adopted by many rehabilitation centers with marked success in restoring the alcoholic to normal life.

That there are strong spiritual and moral dimensions to the problem of alcoholism has long been demonstrated by the phenomenal success of Alcoholics Anonymous, and is newly credited by Dr. George Vaillant, a Harvard psychiatrist, whose book The *Natural History of Alcoholism: Causes, Patterns, and Paths to Recovery* (Cambridge, 1983) is hailed as a landmark study of alcoholism. Vaillant maintains that the "natural healing processes" relieving suffering and creating hope are best fostered today by A.A. Thus he recommends as a first step to sobriety an acceptance of the first precept of A.A.: "I am powerless over alcohol." A.A. works, he says. It works "for sophisticated Harvard-educated loners as well as for gregarious blue-collar workers."

Incidentally, Vaillant also emphasizes the distinction made by Davies that alcoholism is not a sin, not some psychological symptom, not some vague unnamed metabolic riddle, but a disease. "The task," he writes, "is to convince the patient not that he or she *is* an alcoholic, but that he or she is a decent person who has an insidious disease—a disease that is highly treatable but, like diabetes, requires a great deal of responsibility from the patient."

It is counsel to bear in mind in approaching anyone in the family with the problem.

Alcoholism and the Power of Religion

Those encountering alcoholism in the family for the first time should be aware that one of the first casualties to the disease is the individual's spiritual life. The woman, for instance, who takes to alcohol after the death of her husband, may have been a devout person from childhood; now she may grow careless, indifferent, maybe hostile to religion. It is a phenomenon encountered time and again, and Episcopalian Father Gene Geromel writes about it in the Claretian Publications booklet *How the Church Can Help Alcoholics* (Chicago, 1978). He tells of one alcoholic whose lifelong habit of prayer was altered the first time he got drunk. All his life this person had begun the day with prayer. But the morning after his first drunk he could not bring himself to pray. As his alcoholism progressed, prayer ceased to be a part of his life. In fact, he no longer believed in God.

"Fortunately," writes Geromel, "as sobriety returns, spiritual growth can begin. In fact, spiritual growth is a prime requisite for continued sobriety." Not only is spiritual life recoverable, but when it returns it can be stronger than ever. As Geromel says: "One of the most striking things that recovering alcoholics can share with others in the church is their belief in an active, dynamic God. There are few Pelagians in A.A. Its members have experienced God's healing power in dramatic, often miraculous ways. They know it is the power of God which gave them back their life. Few believe that they had much to do with their own rebirth. In a culture and a church where many members assume that human beings make decisions and act through their own power, it is refreshing to meet people for whom God is an active, intervening reality."

Geromel speaks, of course, as a cleryman, but even someone like Harvard's Dr. Vaillant grants that a power greater than one's self can be operative in an alcoholic's case. "Recovery," Vaillant has commented in *Time* magazine, "occurs through a series of events coming together." One is that alcoholics usually need some kind of substitute for alcohol, like tranquilizers, or psychotherapy, or a support group of people with similar problems. Further, he added, "even though it's terribly unscientific, alcoholics usually do seem to need some kind of source of hope and self-esteem, or religious inspiration—whatever you want to call it—and that seems more important than hospital or psychiatric care."

Still, what Geromel calls "an active, dynamic God," and what Vaillant more vaguely calls "religious inspiration" cannot of itself do the whole job. The individual must be willing to help himself or herself—and others in the family, notably adult children, must be willing to assume a degree of responsibility too in instances of senior alcoholism. A higher power may indeed work through A.A., but the person with the problem must be gotten first to A.A. It is a point for the adult child to bear in mind. This might translate to the exerting of pressure. It might mean a chauffeuring chore. But love and concern should override timidness or inconvenience.

A final detail to remember with respect to an aged parent's drinking: Tolerance to alcohol diminishes with age. The older one is, the more vulnerable that person to the effects of alcohol. The aged parent might not be aware of that fact of physiology; it is the adult child's duty to make him or her aware once the trace of a problem shows itself.

Chapter 7

WIDOWHOOD

Preparing to be Alone

IT is an unhappy fact, but one day one or the other of one's aging parents is going to die, and because women live longer than men on the average (by 8.3 years), chances are that it is the father who will die first and the mother who will be left to cope. United States Bureau of Census figures bear out this likelihood. Bureau statistics show that after age 65, less than half of the women of the country still have living spouses.

The implications of these figures are tremendous, and suggest the advisability of preparation for widowhood, both in psychological and practical ways. Actually the psychological preparation is likely to take care of itself, for psychological preparation is an ongoing process. The death of one's spouse is invariably a shock, an occasion of great distress. But the survivor is usually conditioned, at least to some subtle degree, for the loss. The spouse may have been in declining health for some time or may have suffered from a terminal illness; if not that, then the death of the spouses of friends may have set off thoughts about one's own potential widowhood. In any case, the married person who has not thought on occasion of the possibility of being left alone through death is rare. The person, on the other hand, who has taken provision against the day by educating herself or himself in roles which custom or practice assigns to the spouse of the opposite sex is even rarer.

It is as though an insurance policy or survivor's benefits on some pension plan took care of all looming problems. They do not.

If the husband dies first, the widow may immediately be called upon to assume the unfamiliar roles of money manager, handy*man,* or worker in the marketplace. A surviving husband, in turn, may be called upon to be housekeeper, cook, grocery shopper—jack of all chores around the house. If either waits until the other is dead to begin to learn something about the spouse's roles, the person is likely to be overwhelmed. The time to start preparation for widowhood is when the two are alive and one or the other can provide the necessary coaching.

Prudent is the woman who knows how to balance the checkbook; who learns with her husband the tedious income-tax business; who brushes up on her work skills, just in case she has to go out one day and get a job. Wise is the man who learns how to operate the stove, change the bedding, vacuum a carpet. Familiarity with life's small but essential details, of which these are but a few, will make coping that much easier, when coping becomes necessary.

Adult children can assist in this process by suggesting role-sharing ideas to the parents and being able to offer examples from their own marital arrangements.

The Need for a Will

The average American working person puts in some 80,000 hours on the job during his or her lifetime over a span of 45 to 55 work-years. Often the result is the accumulation of assets—house, car, stocks and bonds, furniture, *objects d'art,* etc.—with a value ranging from many thousands of dollars into perhaps hundreds of thousands of dollars. Admittedly, for some this may be accidental, even intangible wealth, wealth that is the direct result of inflation and in nonfluid form. But it is wealth nonetheless. As an example, that modest home that an older couple may have purchased 30 years ago for $20,000—a substantial sum back then—is probably worth five times that amount today, and if so, the couple owning it are one-tenth millionaires! Imagine being one-tenth millionaires!

The astonishing corollary, however, is that people—though worth more—are nevertheless extremely delinquent about drawing up wills. According to a Kennedy-Sinclaire Company survey, seven out of eight Americans die without the benefit of a will. They hold back—some out of a superstition linking wills to death; some out of misinformation, such as the belief that only rich people need wills. Many in the latter category do not appreciate that the inflation of the past decade has actually made them rich persons.

It is unwise not to have a will, says William T. Buckley, a Worcester, Massachussets, attorney who has been practicing law for 44 years. "People should have wills so that their estates may be distributed in accordance with their wishes. If there is no will, the decedent's property is distributed among his or her relatives in accordance with the statutory laws of descent and distribution. If there are no relatives and no will, then the property could go to the state. While the statutory laws are based on how people in general have disposed of their property in the past, they may or may not coincide with the decedent's wishes. For instance, the individual may wish to provide for charitable bequests or bequests to nonrelatives. Without a will, these and other special provisions are impossible, absent a living trust or other testamentary document."

Many older persons, it appears, decide against drawing up a will because their property and bank accounts are held in joint ownership, usually one's spouse. Thus, when one party dies, sole ownership automatically passes to the other party without any necessity for further dispostion. Many persons regard this as provision enough, but as Buckley comments, "What if there is a common disaster and the two die together? Or what if the surviving spouse dies soon after, before having made new and separate provisions? Once again then it is the law which will determine how the estate is to be divided."

"Everyone should have a will," concludes Buckley. "It avoids complications; it speeds up the probate or settlement process; but most especially it gives you control over what you have and own."

It is not easy for children of any age to inquire into matters so personal as a will, even with one's own parents. But in an age when properties have taken on new values due to inflation, and when someone's estimate of these values may be rooted in Depression-era or post-World War II appreciations of money, then the children are advised to press the issue of a will, even at the risk of having one's interest misunderstood as selfishness or avariciousness.

Also, let both aged parents and advising children beware the homemade will, and have the will drawn up by an attorney. Whatever popular books may say on the subject, wills are complex procedures. Further, they are subject to laws that differ from state to state. A will drawn up on the kitchen table and filed away in the desk drawer might have as much standing in court as a barbecue recipe. It may be totally invalid, with the result that the court will end up disposing of one's property. Is there anyone who does not wish to make his or her own decision about the disposition of property owned or possessions held?

The wise course in almost every case is to have a good lawyer draw up one's will. The cost should not be particularly high, and may be as little as thirty-five dollars for an uncomplicated will. Once drawn up, the will should be kept in a safe place, and this information known to someone besides oneself. Many persons keep their will in a safety deposit box at a bank, but there can be much red tape involved in opening the safety deposit box after a person has died. This is a detail that can complicate or negate certain instructions contained in the will, such as funeral arrangements, disposal of vital organs, etc. The person wishing to be buried in the old home town, or desiring to leave vital organs to a medical school or hospital may end up being cremated in the big city with no humanitarian use being made of the organs, all because the heirs or executors could not get the will out of the safety deposit box in time.

The best advice is to leave a copy of one's will (or the original while retaining a copy) with one's lawyer. Or, as is possible in some states upon payment of a small fee, file the will in the office of the Register of Probate or similar office. The will then will be speedily available to those who must make decisions.

Finally, those who make wills should be encouraged to review and update them every two or three years because of periodic changes in family structure, business, and/or state and federal laws.

Incidentally, under the new federal law, the unified gift and estate tax exemption increases from $275,000 in 1983 to $325,000 in 1984; to $400,000 in 1985; to $500,000 in 1986; and to $600,000 in 1987 and later years. Charitable gifts and bequests remain fully deductible, no matter how large.

The Reality of Widowhood

When one or the other parent dies, adult children must of course be of help—by assuming, but ideally only temporarily, responsibilities of the deceased spouse, to the extent necessary and possible; by strengthening child-parent bonds so that there will be a supportive intergenerational relationship at least through the period of adjustment; by providing the listening ear and something of the counsel that once was furnished by the spouse. A fundamental piece of advice: Urge one's parents to postpone for a year or so all major decisions, as with investments or change of residence. A year can make all the difference in the world, and it will take that long for the surviving spouse to adjust and be able to know clearly what he or she would be best doing. Minor mistakes can be corrected or written off; a major mistake could haunt the surviving spouse the rest of a lifetime.

One common impulse when death comes to a family is for the adult child to advise the surviving parent to move— get away from old memories; get a smaller house; move into an apartment. Maybe this is indeed the best of advice. On the other hand, it could be the worst, for it is a very chancy thing to change too much too quickly. Dislocating people from their old environment, taking them away from familiar surroundings, from friends and community could compound the individual's sense of loss and add measurably to the job of coping and adjusting. The old house, the old neighborhood become part of a person's very being, and to sever a surviving parent from these touchstones of life at the very time that he or she is putting together the pieces after the death of a spouse could terribly complicate that person's existence. The surviving parent should be left in familiar surroundings at least for the time being.

Similarly, it is instinctive for a surviving parent to turn to the adult children in time of bereavement, but adult children should beware against encouraging too much dependency. Let them advise; let them listen sympathetically to the widowed parent; let them relieve the loneliness; let them join in activities enriching to the surviving parent; let them be a part of the decision making. But unless there are mitigating circumstances of health or incompetence, let them not encourage utter dependence. This could be physically and psychologically debilitating for the parent. At the same time, the child may be saddling himself or herself with unnecessary and burdensome responsibilities. Death is a tragedy, but there are still lives to be led.

The Specter of Loneliness

There's no question that loneliness is one of the most common problems facing older people. A recent British survey, for instance, identified loneliness as the most common complaint among Britons over 65. Forty-five percent rated it a more difficult problem than lack of money, poor health, family differences, or any other factor in their lives. What is true in England is, or seems to be, no less true in the United States.

Chicago Tribune columnist Bob Greene has told of a 78-year-old widower who wrote to him requesting information about an obscene-telephone-call club that Greene had criticized in his column. The letter intrigued Greene. He sensed a tone different from the deluge of letters re-

ceived in response to the column, and his journalistic instincts told him that there was more behind the request
than a desire to be titillated or erotically aroused.

He called the man up, though he was half-a-continent
away, and he found himself talking to a sincere, gracious,
intelligent individual, who, it turned out, had never made
an obscene telephone call in his life. Why had he written
Bob Greene with a request for information? The answer
was sad and moving.

"Well, I'm alone. I'm past the age when I could go out
to a bar and play kneesies with the girls. I watch the boob
tube, I cook my own meals, I do my own housekeeping—I
sit here like a piece of cheese. I have perhaps half a dozen
beers and three or four cocktails during a year. I drink
almost nothing. I exercise, and I try to live a healthy life,
and I hope to live another ten years. But I am very lonely."

In his loneliness, the man was willing to reach out to an
obscene-telephone-call-club in the hope that after the ob-
scenities had been spent, the person at the other end of the
line would be willing to talk on a regular, normal basis
about life in general. With singular appropriateness, the
Tribune headline writer captioned Greene's column:
"Sometimes loneliness can be obscene, too."

Loneliness has many faces, and for most persons one of
its most gruesome is after the death of one's spouse. The
recently widowed person is lonely for companionship, for
affection, for someone to organize the day with and
around. Most of us at some time in our lives have to learn
to live with a measure of loneliness, but for the new widow
and new widower the problem can be especially difficult.

The adult child can relieve a parent's loneliness by frequent visits and regular telephone calls or letters. If the
loneliness is very severe and if it tends to persist, perhaps

professional counseling may be necessary, or group therapy. To talk out one's problems with others who have undergone a similar experience is always useful. It is also less expensive than individual counseling or therapy, a consideration for those with limited incomes.

One thing: Loneliness should not be coddled.

In that context, let me share a loneliness cure that originated with a St. Cloud, Minnesota, senior citizens' group and which made its way into the weekly bulletin of the parish community of St. Joseph in Minneapolis. The cure, prescribed by Lynn Walters, is based on the idea that no one has the right to complain about loneliness unless he or she has first:

• done at least one kindness for someone who is worse off;

• telephoned at least three people during the past week to find out how they are getting along;

• made plans to do at least one thing with someone else;

• invited at least three people to drop around and say hello;

• checked the local newspaper to see what is going on in town that appeals or looks interesting, then getting out and going to it;

• offered to keep a young child so that a busy mother can get away for a few hours;

• put his or her mind to work learning something on a subject about which it had been thought, "I wish I knew more about that";

• become better acquainted with the local public library.

Walters wound up her reflection with this cogent observation: "Everyone gets lonely sometimes. It happens more to us because we have frequently outlived some of the people we care about. But for anyone to suffer from loneliness is needless. The nicest part of the cure is that it works not only for you, but for someone else as well."

Love Is Not Just for the Young

Not long ago, a friend of mine traveled to Cincinnati to help celebrate her widowed grandfather's 80th birthday. That wasn't all. Next day there would be an even grander ceremony. Grandfather would get married again after having been alone for almost ten years.

"Everyone in the family is happy about the marriage now," my friend conceded recently, but candor impelled her to add that it was not easy to come to that position. "For one thing," she said, "my grandfather lives a thousand miles from the rest of us, and somehow the family had come to think he was at an age where he couldn't make decisions like this for himself. Also, he has a good bit of money, and some of us, I guess, were suspicious that the woman was marrying him for that reason."

Well, of course, there are people, old as well as young, who marry for money, but that was not the case in this instance. My friend's new grandmother-in-law was anything but an avaricious opportunist. A widow herself, she was of an age with her new spouse—73. And she had a healthy bank account of her own. She and the grandfather were doing what so many other widowed people are doing nowadays late in life: remarrying and, odds are, remarrying happily Certainly for my friend's grandfather this proved to be the case. By my friend's delighted admission, her grandfather is happier now than at any time in the ten years since his first wife died.

The trend among elderly single people to marry is a quite

decisive one in the United States. Once upon a time, older single people vegetated in creaky old homes or small apartments, or stayed tucked away in rooms supplied by a caring son or daughter. But now, in an age when people are encouraged to live life to its fullest for as long as possible, older single people are taking a step that not long ago would be branded by many as silly or frivolous. "Look at the old geezer getting remarried," an aunt of mine used to say of widowers of her generation who marched down the aisle in their advanced years. It was a common enough expression, but it is one seldom heard today, either about widowers or remarrying widows.

Statistics reveal why. Marriage among old people has become a commonplace. In the United States, the number of brides 65 or older increased from 7,800 in 1960 to 16,400 in 1973. Records on 2.2 million marriages in 1977 show that 21,180 brides and 38,820 bridegrooms were 65 or older. In 1981 the number of marriages in the 65-and-over age group were estimated at some 80,000. Inevitably some of these were first marriages, and some others followed a divorce. But the vast majority of the marriages involved individuals who were remarrying after widowhood—some 90 percent in the instance of the 1977 figures.

Dirty old men? Giddy old women? Not on your life. Social yardsticks indicate that mostly these were people who had enjoyed happy, long-term marriages, and were anxious to live out their lives in a similarly rewarding relationship. Monsignor Paul W. Clunan, vicar general of the Diocese of Memphis, summed the matter up succinctly in an *Our Sunday Visitor* interview: "The people who had really good marriages are the first ones who want to get remarried when their partner dies. They know how rewarding and warm and good marriage can be, and they have no fears about entering into such a state again."

In point of fact, apart from having the apprehension that is normal with any new step in life, there is no reason for automatic opposition to the remarriage of older persons—and no reason to be unduly pessimistic about the marriage's chances of success. Such a marriage seems to have a statistically better chance of succeeding than the marriage their grandchild is likely to contract. At least so it would seem based on the "Portrait of America" *Newsweek* presented in its January 17, 1983, issue. According to it, half of the children born in 1983 will have to live through their parents' divorces. Divorces of course occur in the remarried aged group, but on nothing like a one-in-two basis.

Barbara Vinick, a Boston University sociologist, has studied the experience of older women who married in later life, and her findings support the proposition that late marriage is anything but a negative thing. She interviewed 24 couples, most of whom had lost spouses in death, and had remarried at ages ranging from 60 to 84. They had been remarried from two to six years at the time of the interviews, in the 1970s. Dr. Vinick found that more than 75 percent of the women were either "very satisfied" or "satisfied" with their new marriages. The same seemed true for the men, although it was women who were the essential focus of the study. Both considered companionship to be the best feature of their marriage, with "touching, holding, intimacy, and the warmth of another body" also important facets of their relationship.

Dr. Vinick found that older-age marriages have several things working for them to create a "calmness and seren-

ity" that could be lacking in marriages between young people. These included freedom from stresses of child rearing,
freedom from in-law conflicts, and a harnessed or re-
strained ambition for higher status. Her conclusion was
that remarriage for older women, and by projection older
men, should be encouraged, and she called on professionals to help offset the old social sterotype that "people
are too old to remarry, don't need to, or shouldn't."

In her book *I Never Feel Old* (Cincinnati, 1981), Frances
Caldwell Durland, an 88-year-old, shared her positive approach to the challenges of aging and told of addressing a
workshop on aging and being abruptly asked the question:
"How do you feel about remarrying?" The question
amused her, and her spontaneous reaction was, "At 87 I
don't think I have much choice." This elicited a laugh, and
another when she added, "Unless, of course, I marry a
much younger man." Turning serious, she reflected: "But
if I were a lot younger, say 20 years, I would marry again if
the right man came along. I like being married.

"Many older couples do marry—some in their 70s and
80s. If a person has kept flexible, alive, and vibrant, I see
no reason for not marrying. Love is not just for the young.
Older people have learned so many lessons about life that
if there is any congeniality of the spirit the marriage is
much less troubled by the problems the young face."

Edwina Hackett, coordinator of the geriatrics program
for the Mid-Town Mental Health Center in Memphis,
sums things up perfectly: "One should keep living as fully
as possible until one dies. And living with a partner is part
of living for many aged people."

When Mom or Dad Start Dating

"Who're you going out with tonight? What time are you
going to be in?"

Those are questions that once would be directed exclusively from parent to child. Today, with so many people living to older age—life expectancy is 69.9 for men and 77.6 years for women, according to 1983 figures of the Department of Health and Human Services in Washington—they are questions often directed from child to parent, as the surviving partner to a marriage begins to explore marital alternatives to widowhood.

What happens when one's parents start dating again?

To begin with, it is more likely that it is Dad who will be doing the dating, for the field is his, so to speak. Due to sex differences in mortality rates, there are almost three single women for every unmarried man in the population over age 65; there are 5.3 times more widows than there are widowers. Said another way, for every 100 men aged 65, there are 134 women, and this ratio difference widens year by year until at age 85 there are 160 women for every 100 men. This means that it is much more probable that the older man will remarry than the older woman. Thus some statistics for 1979: 77 percent of older men were married, as compared to 52 percent of older women.

But for many older persons, male or female, male-female proportion ratios can be much less of a problem than certain other difficulties, many of them right in their own family. When older persons return to dating they encounter troubles unknown when they dated as youths. They encounter prejudice and ignorance about their needs, interference from their children, even denials that they can make decisions any longer. As David Guttmann, director of the Catholic University of America's Center for the Study of Preretirement and Aging, has worded it, it is often the older person's own children "who have ideas about what is appropriate social behavior for their parents." The adult children feel they have the right to ap-

prove or disapprove how their parents lead their lives—
their friends, their lifestyle, their dating, their decision to
remarry.

To be sure, much of this concern—all of it in some
cases—may be sincere and honest, born of love and
fostered by a desire to have happen what is best for the
parent. So, of course, many adult children are quite happy
to see their mother or father date and remarry. It might be
an answer to loneliness, to economic instability. It might
be a means of double-dipping into a happiness, which had
died with one's earlier spouse and which all had thought
had fled forever. In the purely personal context of the
child, it might be relief from worry about one's older
parent's being alone most of the time. Now there is someone else with him or her, and that can be the lifting of a
great worry.

But not all children approach a parent's decision to date
and remarry with largeness of soul and openness of mind.
They object, and their objections may stem from a variety
of causes: selfishness, overprotectiveness, jealousy, and
most especially concern for one's inheritance: *money*. Sociologists say it is a fact of general human experience that
no disagreements are as destructive of family relationships
as disputes over money or inheritances. They can involve
children and relatives all over the family tree.

The remarrying parent can blunt problems of this sort
by being considerate of the feelings of others in the family
and by sitting down and talking things over carefully. It
may be decided that if there are savings or holdings of considerable size these should be kept separate from any new
joint account. Many sociologists advise this course, if only
for peace and harmony in the family. Of course, if there
are not considerable savings or holdings, or if the intention

of the marrying older couple is to stabilize their socio-economic standing by pooling their resources, then that is another matter. In those instances, the logical course would seem to be to combine savings and other holdings.

Inevitably there are some children who are not going to be satisfied, whatever the older parent does by way of arrangements, and who will mask considerations of selfishness under the guise of concern that mother or father is making a mistake of the heart. They should prepare themselves for a rebuff, for there comes a point at which the marrying older couple must say, "Whose life is this anyway?" Or, more bluntly, "It's none of your business."

Adult children must realize that their parent has not surrendered his or her life just because of happening to be advanced in years. Presuming that the older person knows what he or she is doing—that is, that judgment is not impaired by dementia, alcoholism, or other illness affecting the decision-making processes—then the older person has every right to turn aside unwarranted complaints and unnecessary interference from people who should be leading their own lives, not his or hers.

Children should respect their parent's individuality and accept the principle that the most important consideration in any decision made by the elderly parent is the happiness of the parent. If the decision makes the parent happy, the child should respect it.

Further, the children should trust the remarrying parent's good sense. Chances are that they will be pleasantly surprised, for, as mentioned, the rate of successful marriages is quite high among elderly people. Perhaps this is because the marriages are entered into more realistically. Or perhaps success is built on the experience that older people bring to the new union. Or, perhaps again, it is be-

cause older people tend to marry in their own age group—
although not inevitably so, particularly in the cases of
men, who are not as restricted by social norms as women
seem to be. National Center for Health Statistics recently
showed 20 percent of grooms over 65 marrying women
under 45, whereas only 3 percent of older brides wed men
under 45. Whatever these statistics, the tendency is still
strong for older persons to marry in their own age
category—and often with people of their own religious de-
nomination, since it is often in a church environment that
the new partners first meet, a parish golden-age club or
church-seniors circle. Such factors as these are important,
for compatibilities of age, religion, and interests lessen the
risks of unhappiness and divorce.

"Naturally," as Dr. Ivan I. Suchett-Kaye, a University
of Tennessee visiting professor of geriatric medicine, has
commented, "if she likes art galleries and he likes to take
walks alone and look at the birds and the trees, they won't
have too much in common. But neither would a marriage
of 25-year-olds fare too well if that was the case. They have
to exercise good sense."

Picturing Mom or Dad in Bed with Someone Else

On the wall of a barn that I use as a study is a framed
fragment from a 1759 issue of the *New-York Gazette,*
which claimed to provide "the freshest and most important Advices both Foreign and Domestic." Under a Paris
dateline, the following "Advice" appears: "We learn from
St. Gaudens, the capital of the Nebouzen, that there died
lately in the village of la Barthe de Riviere, in the diocese of
Cominges, a surgeon, named Espagno, aged 112, who exercised his profession till the day of his death. He never
was bloded [sic] or purged, nor ever had any illness,

though he was drunk almost every day. He was twice married; the first time, when he was but 20, and the second time when he was 90. By the last marriage he hath a daughter aged 20, who is married, and hath a child.''

My purpose in citing this story is not to recommend one's getting drunk every day, but to dramatize that getting remarried late in life is not exactly a latter-day phenomenon. Though in the past the numbers might have been fewer, older people have been remarrying from time eternal, and usually—let's be candid—for the same romantic reasons that they married as youths. They are sexual creatures, and even at 90, as Dr. Espagno's story illustrates so graphically, the sexual juices can run. At least on occasion.

Even into their own middle age, when their own sexual activity should tell them something about others, adult children forget this physiological detail with respect to their parents: They remain sexual creatures. It is almost as if they believed their parents ceased being sexual creatures when the last child in the family was born. In any case, they appear to regard sexual activity in their elderly parents as something which, if not impossible, is then unnecessary or just not nice. It is a frame of mind that contributes to the difficulty many people have in understanding why their widowed mother or father might want to marry again. Reasons of loneliness, insecurity, and economic necessity are all much easier to grasp than reasons of romance and physical attraction.

Antoinette Smith, a United Methodist Church marriage counselor in Nashville, is one who has tried to counter this almost monastic way of thinking. She has called on churches and synagogues to realize that people are "sexual from birth to death," and to recognize that older people, to be specific, are not "asexual." They have sexual feelings, needs, and desires that are natural, healthy, and God's good gift, and helping older persons to meet sexual needs is a means "of fulfilling a basic need for all persons for intimacy and love."

Her plea did not go unanswered. It was made in Pittsburgh at a consultation sponsored by the National Council of Churches, the American Association of Retired Persons, and the National Retired Teachers Association, and the consultation recommended that the human sexuality needs of older persons be included in ministerial education, church institutions, and in local programing. Thus at the organizational level something is being done.

On the level of individuals, however, old attitudes seem to be prevailing, and particularly among sons and daughters vis-à-vis their parents. They can be very understanding about the decisions of other older people to marry, but when it comes to their own parents, it is as if the issue were another matter entirely. They find it hard to reconcile themselves to the thought of their widowed mother or father climbing into bed with someone else other than their old partner.

Well, those who have problems about a parent's remarrying had better brace themselves, as the sexuality issue is broadening in ways they may hardly imagine possible. For the new morality is touching the older generation just as certainly as it has the young and middle-age generations. The *New York Times* pointed up that fact with a Thanksgivingtime story in 1982, entitled "Thoroughly Modern Grandma: Good Jobs and Jogging Suits." One of the grandmothers featured was a woman divorced and living with a man in Brooklyn. Her son and daughter-in-law were "scandalized" by this arrangement, according to the

Times, and "would rather the grandchildren not visit her." The children, however, insisted on visiting, and the grandmother and her "best friend" apparently loved this. They would take the children to arty films and to sushi bars. They taught them to play poker. How old is the grandmother? Fifty-seven. "Just call me the Sensuous Grandmother," she said to the *Times.*

There is no moral to that story, only the message that older people are still sexual people. Obviously this applies to homosexual as well as heterosexual older people, as a notice read recently made clear. It announced a conference on lesbian and gay aging, sponsored by the National Association of Lesbian and Gay Gerontologists. Now presumably one's mother is not a lesbian and one's father is not a homosexual, but whether they are or not, they are sexual creatures, widowed or not. The adult child should not forget this when Mom or Dad announces plans to be remarried.

Remarriage and Social Security Benefits

Once upon a time, remarriage after age 60 could seriously diminish one's Social Security benefits, and in protecting their income many individuals were confronted with the choice of breaking off their romance or moving in with their partner without benefit of clergy, as they say—a decision which cut against the moral grain of many belonging to a generation which was taught to frown on cohabitation. President Jimmy Carter resolved many of these difficulties, however, by signing into law, December 20, 1977, significant amendments to the Social Security Act. Now widows and widowers over age 60 are able to remarry and not suffer a reduction in their Social Security survivors' benefits. They are entitled to receive benefits on their deceased spouses' account equal to the benefit their spouses would have received if still alive. If the new spouse gets Social Security benefits, the individual may elect to take a dependent's benefit on the new spouse's work record if that benefit would be larger.

The rule regarding remarriage does not apply to people under 60 or to those receiving benefits as a surviving divorced spouse. Remarriage would make such a person ineligible for such benefits. If the subsequent marriage ends, though, the widow under 60 or the surviving divorced spouse may become entitled to a dependent's benefit on the deceased spouse's work record.

One other piece of Social Security information is worth remembering: Prior to the enactment of the 1977 amendments, Social Security recipients were limited to earnings of $3,000 a year without a reduction in benefits. This ceiling has been raised over the years. As of January 1, 1983, Social Security beneficiaries under the age of 65 may earn $4,920 without affecting their benefits, and those over 65 may earn $6,600. These annual exempt amounts are likely to increase in future years to keep pace with increases in average wages.

If one's earnings exceed the annual exempt amount, one dollar in benefits will be withheld for each two dollars of earnings above the exempt amount.

The Social Security Act is a complex package of legislation, subject to frequent revision from Congress to Congress, as the major revisions enacted in 1983 make plain. People of Social Security age are advised to keep in close touch with their Social Security office, so as to be up-to-date on their eligibility and benefits. Even in quiet legislative years small changes could be implemented which could radically affect one's Social Security standing.

The Social Security Administration maintains a toll-free telephone service for the answering of inquiries, but a more advisable way of keeping in touch is by visiting one's local or area Social Security office, where officials are on hand to respond to questions. While there, one should be sure to review the Social Security Administration literature laid out on display tables or in pamphlet racks. Adult children and people on Social Security may be surprised to find that they are eligible for a range of benefits of which they had no idea. This is a sampling of pamphlets I picked up on my last visit: "Medicare for People with Permanent Kidney Failure," "SSI for Aged, Disabled, and Blind People," "Your Social Security Rights and Responsibilities—Retirement and Survivors Benefits," "A Brief Explanation of Medicare," "Home Health Care Under Medicare," and, of special interest to the young-olds, a booklet entitled "Thinking of Retiring?"

Retirement Communities: Bane or Blessing?

Raymond Smith is 50; a bachelor; a member of a religious community. His mother is 80, widowed, and remarkably vigorous. She travels widely—indeed is just recently back from China. A few years ago, she visited the Middle East. She lives in New Jersey, but she gets to the theater in New York City several times a year. She goes out to lunch and dinner with some frequency during the week. She takes continuing-education courses, and goes to church meetings. There is always something going on. But Smith's mother wants to move into a retirement community. He opposes the idea strenuously.

The attractions of the retirement community for Mrs. Smith are the usual ones: more extensive peer contacts and quieter and more orderly living arrangements. These are strong inducements for a woman who lives on the eleventh floor of an apartment building in a downtown city area that is neither particularly attractive nor quiet. In addition, this retirement community has its own nursing home so there is the assurance of guaranteed care, if and when the day arrives that this is necessary.

The son is unpersuaded. For him there is something irrevocable and antigenerational about retirement communities, and something selfish. He could have been thinking of the Arizona retirement community which advertised: "The community is like a small town with no schools, no hot rods, no monopolization of recreational facilities by youngsters." But Smith's principal objection, one that persons in situations similar to his and his mother's might bear in mind, is that retirement communities, by segregating themselves to whatever degree from the rest of society, diminish the intergenerational contacts which we all need for intellectual and psychological stimulation.

This is a point that Margaret Mead, the late and eminent anthropologist, used to make in a slightly different context. She judged it one of the tragedies of American life that people are cast aside when they become old. Yet with retirement communities, it is not a case of older people being cast aside; it is a case of older people doing to themselves what society was once criticized for doing to them: segregating them.

I would like to submit another consideration: Older people have so much to give to society that it is socially inadvisable for them to cut themselves off from the mainstream of community life. They deprive the rest of society culturally. Margaret Mead reinforced this observation by noting the effects of age-segregation on young people. Young people, she said, grow up culturally impoverished when they do not have contact with grandparents and others who belong to their grandparents' generation; they tend to lack a sense of lived history and biological continuity. Older people in turn impoverish themselves culturally when they wall themselves off from those of the other generations.

None of the foregoing is meant as an outright condemnation of retirement communities. They can be very pleasant places, and very many elderly persons are enormously happy in them, although the degree of happiness and the facility with which individuals adjust to them may be predicated on background. A University of Miami study has found, for instance, that lifelong area residents were happier in their old neighborhoods. However, more transient individuals, retirees migrating to Florida, were more satisfied living in retirement communities than in traditional neighborhoods.

If the older persons are convinced that they can be happier in a retirement community, fine. It can be a comfort to adult children to know that their elderly parents are located in housing that is clean, decent, and well-protected, and also that they are with other elderly people whose company they can enjoy. It is a comfort too for society to know that, at a time when there are so many elements of the population to worry about, at least one part of one group—and a vulnerable one at that—is fending well for itself. On the other hand, it is important to know that these consolations come at a price: to the retirement-community member in terms of less stimuli; to the rest of us in terms of cultural loss. Persons who go into retirement communities deprive the rest of us of their presence, their gifts. If this seems a minor loss, think again. Think of artists like Fritz Eichenberg, poets like Robert Frost, doctors like John Rock, scientists like Albert Einstein—think of your own grandparents. And ask if the world would be just as enriched a place, and memories as cherished, if all the aging had taken themselves off at age 65 for Sun City, U.S.A.

Chapter 8

WHEN HEALTH GOES

Hostile Parent, Perplexed Child

CONFLICTS between parents and their children are as old as Genesis. They can also be chronic. They can ease or even seem to disappear, when the children go off on their own to start their own families, only to rekindle themselves in old age, when alteration of the dependency equation brings the once contentious family members back in close contact one with the other. In such instances, children of conflict have a lifetime of experience on which to draw and can act in their maturity as adult children, *not* children forever expected to obey whatever the parent says or do whatever the parent orders. Some parents never seem to acknowledge that their children have grown up, and they seek to keep them under their thumb all their lives. Adult children who let this happen to them are foolish. Parents are to be honored, but not forever obeyed. The reins are off once the child is an adult, unless of course there are exceptional circumstances. For instance, parents obviously can maintain some control as long as they continue to provide financial support. Nevertheless, the best rule is for aged parents to treat their adult children as friends— friends of a very special kind to be sure—rather than children or minors. The adult child has a right to demand this.

Conversely, some adult children will enjoy a blissful intergenerational relationship with their parents through childhood, through young adulthood, into middle age, then find the whole thing slipping away. It is an experience that can leave the adult son or adult daughter badly unsettled.

Mary N. of Brooklyn is a case in point. Her 80-year-old mother was in a nursing home, and Mary made a point of seeing her every other day. Trouble was, the visits were a disaster. There would be arguments, displays of hostility, and Mary would depart drained and depressed. At 55, she did not need this aggravation. Take what happened recently: It was a lovely spring day, and the caretaker-gardener was pruning an apple tree in the yard behind the nursing home. "Look at Father out there trimming the apple tree," said the aged mother. "Mom," replied the daughter, "that is not Father. Father died in 1971. This is 1983. And that is not your back yard. You're in Wartburg Lutheran Home." The mother reacted briskly and with accusations about the daughter's love and feelings towards her parents. The daughter calmed the mother before she left, but that did not help her own migraine headache. She went home and fought with her family.

Raymond R. Johnson, director of social services at Wartburg Lutheran Home for the Aged in Brooklyn, offers the Mary N. case as an example demonstrating how poor communication between aged persons and their children can result in hostility between the parties. In this instance, the aged mother was living in a fantasy world, and the daughter's correction amounted to a confrontation. Either the aged mother was lying or the daughter was lying. The mother was sure that she was right in her observation, so the daughter herself was lying, trying to delude the mother for whatever fancied purpose.

Psychological history in the main validates the

daughter's approach. Orientation therapy—that is, the orienting of the mentally confused to the present situation—has long been in vogue. But a whole new school of thought has arisen which holds that when an aged person is expressing a fantasy, that person is doing it for a reason, and one should be very sure about one's action before challenging that reason. Thus we have what is known as validation therapy—the theory that one validates the aged person's fantasy, because it exists for a reason, and also because to correct the fantasy is to risk hostility on the part of the aged person, or to risk injury to the person's spirits by convincing her that she is wrong. Or him, as the case may be.

None of this is a call to the children of aged parents to choose between therapeutic approaches, and become practitioners of medicine, as it were. However, to improve communication they are advised to consult with a geriatrician, a doctor who specializes in medicine for the elderly, or with a psychologist—and if the parent is in a nursing home they should attend the seminars and in-service training sessions that many homes hold for the children of the institutionalized aged on how to communicate with loved ones. A world of problems could be solved.

Whatever one does, one should not assume that hostility or abusiveness towards children on the part of aged parents is a permanent state. Johnson maintains that 70 percent of the time this is not true, and that often all that is needed is adjusted medical care and more knowledgeable communication on the part of the children.

Most emphatically Johnson warns against ascribing confusion, hostility, or abusiveness on the part of the aged to "senility." In fact, he cautions on the very use of the word. "All senile means is to be old," comments Johnson.

"It is not a pejorative word, or at least should not be. Senile dementia is the problem when an old person becomes demented."

Cognitive impairment is today the preferred clinical term for senility, and in the elderly person it requires precise diagnosis. Which is to say that a doctor should be consulted when certain signs evidence themselves: impaired memory, impaired judgment, loss of insight, flattening of affect, change of personality. These could be symptoms of a quite serious illness—perhaps Alzheimer's disease, a scary form of dementia in the elderly (about which more in chapter 9); perhaps multi-infarct disease, or hardening of the arteries caused by atherosclerotic disease.

Alzheimer's disease and multi-infarct disease are the two most frequent causes of dementia in the elderly, Alzheimer's alone claiming over a million victims and some 100,000 lives each year. However, the presence of certain symptoms, such as forgetfulness or quixotic behavior, should not be automatically read as senile dementia; the problem could be caused by any number of other factors— imbalance of medication, for instance, or the wrong medication. This can be diagnosed, and current medical knowledge can be applied to reverse or manage the problems of many elderly persons experiencing cognitive impairment.

The important thing for an individual seeing signs of cognitive impairment in an elderly parent is not to panic, but to consult a doctor or mental health professional. The odds are that the parent can be helped. According to the Duke University Center for the Study of Aging and Human Development, an estimated 5 percent of adults 65 and older suffer severe, chronic, and irreversible cognitive impairment. Another 5 percent exhibit moderate degrees of impairment. This leaves 90 percent of the elderly in control of their cognitive faculties. That is a large group, and puts to rout the old presumption that "senility" inevitably accompanies old age. It just plain is not so. "Senility" is a loaded word, a "wastebasket term," to use Johnson's words, which masks the reality of reversible or at least treatable symptoms among very many of those who one day would have been categorized as demented.

This still leaves of course the difficult aged parent, the parent who is a chronic complainer, who can never be pleased, who remembers the bad and never the good in others, who is demanding and never forgiving. There is a large group of such people out there, but realize they are not all of an age. Persons who are young or middle aged can be just as difficult, just as demanding, just as one-dimensional. Somehow, however, we tend to be more impatient when these qualities are manifested in the aged. How does one cope with those feelings? There is no pat answer—although it is fair to say that an extra measure of love and tact will help, along with a sensitiveness to the point made by Ruth Snow earlier in the book: Aging is no fun thing. Maybe the aged parent should not be complaining. On the other hand, maybe the adult child should not be so impatient either.

Aged and with You

It was a situation almost any American family could find itself in, and be just as perplexed as the McCarty family of Boston.

Mrs. McCarty's mother, Mrs. Espinoza, lived alone for more than 20 years and managed adequately. But now she was 85 and had become confused. The McCarty family took Mrs. Espinoza in, converting the sewing room of their home into a bedroom for her. The complications were immediate. Mrs. Espinoza would roam the house day and night looking for her pocketbook, or her cat, or the bathroom. If she forgot where the bathroom was, she would urinate anywhere. The strain was hard on everyone. Mr. McCarty and the three teenage children were losing sleep at night and being deprived of their privacy during waking hours. Mrs. McCarty became increasingly frustrated at not being able to accept or control her mother's behavior. She slapped her mother's wrists and issued threats seeking to obtain the mother's compliance. Thus, in addition to an inability to cope, the daughter found herself struggling with feelings of guilt for her own behavior. The mother suffered from senile dementia and was disoriented, but Mrs. McCarty did not understand the causes. She was becoming emotionally overwhelmed.

Sister Nancy Vendura of the Daughters of Charity related the case history of the McCartys, a fictitious name but not a fictitious case, in *Charities USA,* and told of its resolution.

Mrs. McCarty was visited by a nurse of the Family-In-Home service, a component of the Family Support for the Aged program sponsored as a pilot project of the Catholic Charitable Bureau of the Archdiocese of Boston. It developed a plan of care for Mrs. McCarty. Mrs. Espinoza's behavior was interpreted for Mrs. McCarty, and reality orientation techniques were demonstrated. The mother's room was rearranged to accommodate a commode, and Mrs. McCarty was instructed in the physical and psychological considerations of using a posey vest, which would safely restrain her mother when it was impossible to watch her closely.

Earlier a doctor had prescribed a tranquilizer for Mrs. Espinoza, indicating senile dementa as her diagnosis. The nurse contacted the doctor, advising him of the situation. He directed adjustment of the tranquilizer dosage, as Mrs. Espinoza's condition would indicate. In collaboration with the doctor, the nurses made appropriate medication dosage increments, and directed the McCarty family towards Mrs. Espinoza's stabilization by educating them to the purpose, dosage, administration times and methods. The nurses explained the side effects of the medication to them, described the warning signs, and gave instructions about when the family should notify them.

The results were rewarding. Mrs. Espinoza became much calmed. The constant questioning and activity noticeably diminished. Mrs. Espinoza was sleeping at night and so was the McCarty family. Before retiring, Mrs. McCarty would wake her mother and assist her to the commode, and return her to bed safely vested for the night.

In the daytime hours, Mrs. McCarty no longer strained as before to hear and respond to her mother's mumblings, but interacted with her in more fruitful fashion by phrasing statements concretely so that her mother could respond to simple directions. Planned activities such as gardening, dish-washing, and folding clothes were mutually therapeutic. Mrs. McCarty felt more secure in handling her mother, had enormously more patience with her, and decided to keep her mother at home rather than place her in a nursing home.

The McCartys were lucky. They were wise enough to seek professional help, and they knew where to turn. But for every McCarty family there is another that has no notion where to turn and ends up bumbling along, making life frightfully more difficult for everyone, including the aged member of the family.

So the crucial question: Where does a family turn, when

an aged parent or other relative becomes a hardship and a
worry for the household as a whole?

More specifically, where does the family turn whose
need is to learn those principles of management and care
that rescued the McCarty family's home situation? How
does one become familiar with the resources and entitle-
ments that are available for the aged person?

This is vital information to come by, for the instinctive
reaction among some sons and daughters, who themselves
might be 50 or 60 years old, is to think of nursing home
placement when their elderly parent shows signs of decline.
This may not be best, and it certainly is not always
necessary, for a variety of programs exist which duplicate
in the family setting all of the services of the nursing
home—and generally at lesser cost to the family, as well as
to the public treasury. (As much as 88 percent of the average nursing home's costs are picked up through Medicare
or other public payments.)

What are these programs? Well, for one thing, one can
arrange for physical therapists and occupational therapists
to do home visits. Also available are meals-on-wheels,
friendly visiting, light housekeeping, shopping, regular
phone contact, and social-service assistance. (See chapter
10 for detailed listing and descriptions.)

The problem is that many people just do not know
where to turn for help. Often the telephone directory is not
much help, for unless one knows the name of the agency
supplying a particular service, one could hunt forever for
the number to call. A more immediate source is one's doctor, pastor, or rabbi. As professionals in health or family
care and counseling, they know exactly where to go. Senior
citizens centers are likewise good sources, as also are
departments or offices of the aging; a telephone call to city

or town hall will steer the person in the right direction. And don't forget that neighbor who has been through an experience similar to one's own. There is a wealth of information in that source, you can be sure. Finally, United Way. You contribute at the office, right? Well, then, call its information and referral services office. Assistance will be found at the other end of the telephone.

Guilt Trips

The Leonards are a particularly proud New York family, a family of high achievers, of standing in the community, of middle-class means. There are two artists in the family, a lawyer, a priest, and, as is so often the case in families of the Leonard's ethnic background, a daughter who never married, who sacrificed career and marriage prospects to take care of Mother. The problem was that Mother was virtually indestructible. She lived on and on, and in very good health. But then the inevitable began to occur. Mother began to show the signs of age. She experienced sensory changes and had deep feelings of uselessness and bouts of depression. Uncharacteristically, she gave way to hostility and displays of agitation. Her sight began to go, and then muscle control. Mother became incontinent. She was now a 24-hour, total management problem for the unmarried daughter, the last of the five Leonard children at home. The complication was that the daughter at 55 was no longer young herself; she had neither the stamina nor the professional training to cope with the aged parent. Mother would have to go into a nursing home, the daughter decided.

The decision was announced to the brothers and sisters, and all hell broke loose. "Mother will not go into a nursing home. She is going to stay at home," they insisted. "It's cruel. We won't hear of it. This was her home, and she'll die here, not in an institution."

The single daughter tried to abide by their wish, but it soon became apparent that the brothers and sisters were demanding too much. Mother was a major health care, and if she was not placed quickly in a nursing home, the family would have two patients on its hands instead of one. The responsibility for the mother was exacting that great a physical and psychological toll on the daughter.

Through Friends and Relatives of the Institutionalized Aged, a private service organization in the New York area that rates and recommends nursing homes, the Leonard children found a placement for their mother that was clean and reasonable and within convenient visiting distance.

But then came the complication: The family members, and most especially the single daughter, began to experience strong feelings of guilt, as if they had somehow been disloyal to Mother, turning her over to others, abandoning her "when, God help us, we should be caring for her ourselves."

"It is a common form of response," says Raymond Johnson of Wartburg Lutheran Home for the Aged, "and not a particularly valid one." Johnson finds family willingness to take care of the elderly in the home as strong today as ever it has been historically. "When I was at the Bayside Senior Center," Johnson commented with respect of a nearby neighborhood program for the elderly," I thought I would find a lot of people who were isolated or abandoned by family. But I found that 95 percent of the time there was a relative on whom the aged person could rely for love and care. They're around, although it is all too true that they do not necessarily know how to help. Many lack the sophistication to think about social services and

look up a social service agency. But I don't see the aban-
donment of the elderly, the 'old-old', people 80 to 90, by
their children, who are in their 50s, 60s, 70s. Very few people really dissociate themselves from their mother or their
father—although it does happen on occasion."

But guilt is another matter. "Many people feel that they
are abandoning their mother or their father, their husband
or their wife, when they place either or both of them in a
nursing home," Johnson remarks. "It happens even
though it is very clear to them that they have done everything possible and that their last choice for the loved one is
having her or him admitted to a nursing home. But knowing the facts often does not alleviate the feeling of guilt."

Some nursing homes provide counseling to help family
members understand that guilt. Some arrange group therapy sessions, where persons can draw on the experience of
others for mutual support. Such programs can be very
useful in helping adult children come to an understanding
of the guilt felt when an aged parent is placed in a nursing
home.

In this context, a Johnson rule of thumb is worth keeping in mind: Those who experience guilt are generally the
ones without real guilt.

How come?

"Because the person who feels guilt is the person who is
concerned, a person who has tried to do all that could be
done," says Johnson. "It is often the person who does not
feel guilt, who just doesn't give a darn, who should be the
one carrying any burden of conscience."

"Laid-On" Guilt

But there is another kind of guilt feeling, a guilt laid on
by a selfish, embittered, or otherwise malcontent aged par-

ent. The type is familiar enough. It is the aged mother who
is constantly complaining: "You didn't call yesterday.
Weren't you feeling well?" "How come you don't visit me
as often as you used to do? Don't you love me anymore?"
Or it is the aged father who martyr-like volunteers the
comment, "You don't want me to go to the game with
you. I'll only be in the way." Or, "Go along. I'll be fine
here by myself." Or, "That soup you brought me yesterday was delicious, but it gave me the most awful heart-
burn. I hope you didn't give any to the children."

Guilt can also be laid on by other relatives or friends.
Like the cousin who says to you after you've gone through
the agony of placing a parent in a nursing home, "Oh, I
would never do that." Or who tells you, after you have
gone to great trouble to find a nursing home for a parent,
and which you visit every day, "Oh, that home is no
good."

Persons who allow themselves to feel guilt under the
weight of such comments are very silly, for this is not guilt.
The comments are unreasonable, or at the very least unnecessary. As long as an individual is trying to do what he
or she believes is decent and good, and best for the parent,
that person should feel no guilt whatsoever. The intruding
cousin should be told to mind his or her own business.

Similarly, so far as a complaining parent is concerned, it
is not a bad thing to remind the parent on occasion that
you too have a life to lead. This might necessitate saying no
to a parent at times, as when the parent might want to
move in for the summer, or demand that you spend your
vacation at the old home in the country when in fact you
had planned a camping trip to Maine with your own family. A firm no now and then can clear a lot of air, and may
be the best thing for both generations. Your life will still be

yours, and the parents will be put on notice against becoming prematurely or unnecessarily dependent on you. Paradoxically, of the two the greater beneficiary may be to those of the senior generation, for dependency can have debilitating effects. This is a point made before, but one worth repeating. The longer one's parents can lead their own lives, the better off they will be psychologically and perhaps also physically. But so too will adult children be better off when their parents are not directing or controlling their lives.

Choosing a Nursing Home

Several years ago, Raymond M., a bachelor, placed his aged mother in a nursing home operated by nuns. The home was once a magnificent private estate. It overlooked the Atlantic from Maine's north coast, and seemed to have everything the model nursing home should have: caring personnel, fine sleeping quarters, nice dining room, pleasant grounds, opportunities for privacy, and a marvelously relaxing view. The nursing home even had a chapel, for the building had been used as a novitiate back when vocations to religious orders were plentiful. In fact, the nuns purchased the estate as a novitiate, not for use as a nursing home. It was only after vocations to religious life began to dry up in the mid-1960s that they adapted the property as a nursing home for the aged.

For two years, Raymond visited his mother dutifully, and more and more he became troubled. The mother never complained, but he suspected she was not happy there. Further, regular visits to the nursing home opened his eyes to details which had eluded him earlier—with respect to staff, food, safety requirements, such as fire doors. One day he told the mother that he was taking her out of there and moving her to a nursing home in the next town. The mother wept with joy, quite literally. Then it came gushing out. She was miserably unhappy. The aged residents were herded about like they were young novices of the old days. She couldn't pack fast enough.

The story had a happy ending all around. The mother was delighted with her new nursing home, and the son had the quiet satisfaction of reading in the paper some months later that the nursing home had been shut down. State officials on a routine inspection had found the home in violation of a number of regulations, only one of which was the absence of fire doors. The nuns eventually sold the property and went off to another state.

Raymond M.'s experience may not be typical, but it does point up the urgency of selecting a nursing home for one's parent(s) with extreme care. Not only is it easy to make a mistake regarding a nursing home, but to correct that mistake can involve a whole new set of problems, physical and psychological, for the nursing home resident. No one wishes to be a human football, kicked from place to place. But understandably some elderly persons feel they are precisely that after being moved once, twice, maybe a third time—all because those making the placement initially had not done proper investigating into the nursing home and how that home fit the parent's needs.

Some fundamental rules of thumb are in order in choosing a nursing home.

1. Providing that the parent is mentally competent, it is important to involve the parent step by step in the decision-making process. After all, it is the parent, not the adult child who will be living in the facility. Ideally the final choice should be the parent's. In any case, just do not dump an aged parent in a nursing home. The shock could

be traumatic. Some well-intentioned children shield their
aged parents from considerations about a nursing home.
They do not confide with them why the action is necessary.
They do not discuss with them the choices that are available, or the type institution that would be best for them.
They keep it all secret, for the best of intentions, of course.
Then one day they deliver the parent to the nursing
home—perhaps under the pretext of taking her or him for
a ride. If these parents have feelings of rejection, and har-
bor resentments on that account, small wonder. Aged
parents like everyone else deserve the truth, and this applies to nursing home placement as well as anything else.
Tactful honesty on that score will spare a lot of family
grief.

2. Determine quite carefully what kind of nursing home
your parent needs and do not rely completely on your own
instincts or the parent's word, though surely that should be
taken into account. Consult with the parent's physician
and other skilled professionals, such as nurse and social
worker. They will be able to advise whether the older person should be in a Skilled Nursing Facility (SNF) or an Intermediate Care Facility (ICF).

A *Skilled Nursing Facility* is one for individuals requiring 24-hour supervision and care. Such facilities provide
medical care, professional nutritional supervision, diag-
nostic and dental services, occupational and physical
therapy, and the like. If a skilled nursing facility lacks a
standard service, then chances are that it has an arrangement with a nearby hospital, clinic, or other health facility
to avail itself of the service there. This is a point to be
checked, however.

An *Intermediate Care Facility* is for an older person not
needing 24-hour supervision and care. These facilities pro-

vide less comprehensive services and smaller, less-profes-
sional staff, being geared to the resident's routine needs,
social and dietary, rather than to medical and rehabilitation needs.

3. Make a careful determination about nursing home
costs and what you can afford. Care in an intermediate
care facility is considerably less than in a skilled nursing
facility, but both are expensive. In the New York area,
skilled nursing home facilities were averaging $30,000 a
year in 1983. Medicare and Medicaid can relieve a family
of a substantial proportion of nursing home costs, so it is
important in choosing a nursing home to make sure that
the facility is eligible for Medicare and Medicaid funds,
and what the conditions are for the nursing home resident
to qualify for these funds. One's local social services
agency or Social Security office will be able to answer
questions, and the admissions offices of most nursing
homes will help one through the application process. When
a nursing home is found, request that bills be itemized, and
know beforehand if there are extra charges, and for what.

4. Make quite sure that the nursing home is properly
licensed. A license is not an absolute guarantee that a nursing home is a good one, but at least the prospective resident and his or her family know that the home is being in-
spected and at the minimum, meeting required standards.
Licenses to look for would be a state nursing home license,
a nursing home administrator's license, and accreditation
from the American Association of Homes for the Aging
and the American Nursing Home Association. One might
also look for a Joint Committee on Accreditation of Hospitals certificate.

The adult child placing an aged parent should beware of
arrangements whereby a person, generally a nurse, takes

older persons into his or her residence and calls this a nursing home. Such an establishment might provide excellent care. There might be an excellent doctor on 24-hour call. But the limitations of the arrangement, and the risks, make such a placement very chancy.

5. Look around the nursing home before arriving at any decision about placement, and evaluate its qualities in detail. Do not trust word-of-mouth about a nursing home; word-of-mouth can be notoriously unreliable. Also, do not trust impressions gained solely in a front office or lobby. Ask to be shown around, or wander about yourself. Visit a second or third time. Evaluate and form your opinions, and check them out with others who are knowledgeable. In a word, buy a nursing home like you'd buy a used car: carefully. Shop around—and be sure to kick the tires.

Kathleen A. Hughes of the Center for Study of Responsive Law, founded by Ralph Nader, pointed up the importance of choosing a nursing home carefully in an op-ed page article in the July 4, 1983, *New York Times*. The general assumption is that nursing homes have improved dramatically since the so-called "dark days" of the late 1960s, early 1970s. But, said Hughes, nothing could be further from the truth, and she proceeded to describe appalling conditions reported from coast to coast in the last year. California inspectors, she claimed, found "cockroaches and puddles of urine and excrement on the floor" of several nursing homes in the Los Angeles area. And Maryland health officials revoked a home's license because the home was "understaffed, poorly managed, and infested by flies and cockroaches." Added Hughes: "On any given day, according to Federal statistics, nearly one nursing home in three harbors health-threatening conditions. Inspectors cite less serious problems in 46 percent of the country's homes that, unless corrected, would threaten residents' health.''

Hughes' plea was for a strengthening, not a relaxation of public health standards and legally required inspections. But her article, to repeat, serves as warning to everyone to be very careful in choosing a nursing home.

Evaluating a Nursing Home

Evaluation of a nursing home should be no haphazard thing, but should be done systematically and thoroughly— and preferably with notebook in hand, particularly if one is looking into several possibilities. Did you ever go house hunting and, after seeing just a few homes, become confused as to which had what feature and which another? The same can happen in checking into nursing homes. Make a master checklist and record impressions and information for each one separately. Here are some details to be checked:

• *Neighborhood and Facility*

Are visitors welcome, but, more important, is the nursing home conveniently located for family and friends? Nursing-home placement will increase, not diminish, the individual's desire and need for contact with those close and dear. Do not disappoint these by selecting a home that is inordinately out of the way, or in an unsafe neighborhood.

Other considerations are almost exclusively those of the person being placed. Is the nursing home a pleasant place? Are there patios and grounds for the residents' enjoyment in good weather? Those with aged parents who are on crutches, using walkers, or in wheelchairs will want to notice if there are ramps. Are there comfortable chairs in the lounges, recreational rooms? Are there attractive appointments, and patient conveniences, such as water coolers, telephones, canteen, library, adequate toilet rooms? Is there a quiet place where one can go to write a letter or postcard? Will the elevator accommodate a wheelchair?

• *Safety Factors*

Few of us are expert safety inspectors, but in choosing a nursing home there are obvious safety details that the untrained eye can check. The most important are these: fire doors, enclosed stairwells, fire-alarm boxes, automatic sprinkler system, fire-fighting equipment, exit signs, and posted notices of procedures to be followed in cases of emergency. Are they easily visible and strategically located, and are there periodic fire drills for residents and staff for every shift? The nursing home's administrators will undoubtedly be anxious to provide assurances about safety, but the prudent person will confirm with the fire department of the area that inspections have been made and that the home is in fact as safe as safety equipment can make a nursing home.

The conscientious adult child will also be concerned about the nursing home being as accident-proof as possible. Is the place well-lighted throughout? Are there handrails in the hallways, grab bars in showers and toilets? Are tables and chairs solid and firm, or easily tilted? Are stairwell doors kept closed?

Finally, are there bedside call-bells for all residents? Ask to see one demonstrated, and note whether the call-bell rings or lights a signal at the nursing station. Preferably the call-bell will ring, and loud enough so as to attract the attendant's attention if his or her back is turned, or he or she is otherwise distracted. It is important that the call-bell can only be turned off at the bedside of the resident.

• *Living Arrangements*

Of particular importance is the selection of a nursing home that the aged parent will find pleasant and congenial. A mistake in this department could diminish life's attractiveness for the resident, and perhaps set in motion physical and psychological disturbances that could hasten the end for the individual. Everything should be done to make life seem really worth living—still.

Therefore, check:

—*Bedrooms.* Are they spacious, clean, comfortable? What are the mattresses like? Can the beds be raised and lowered when the resident is bed-bound? Is there enough closet and drawer space? Can valuables be secured? Can residents furnish their rooms with personal items, such as a television set or air conditioner?

—*Dining room and service areas.* Is a properly qualified nutritional expert in charge of the food service? Are the meals appetizing and are they freshly prepared (as distinct from frozen)? Are they served on china plates (as distinct from paper plates), and with metal utensils (as distinct from plastic disposables)? Some nursing homes have gone the "convenience-food" route, but the concerned adult child will want to ask if this is what he or she wants for the aged parent: a life lived out eating frozen dinners. It seems an unhappy fate—like being checked into McDonald's for the duration of one's years.

Other points of consideration: Are menus posted, and are the advertised foods actually served? Are residents' food preferences taken into consideration? Is the dining room cheerful, and are the meals unhurried? Can wheelchair residents move conveniently between tables? Are bed-patients fed when necessary? Are between-meal and bedtime snacks available?

Individuals will also want to visit the kitchen area to make sure there is a dishwashing machine (very important), and that the areas are separate for food preparation, dishwashing, and garbage.

• *Staff*

The vital considerations here relate to medical services. Has the nursing home a medical director qualified in geriatric medicine and a nursing director similarly qualified? Is a doctor on call at all times and a registered nurse on duty at all times? How regularly is the nursing home resident checked by both? May residents be allowed to have their own physician attend them? What of the practical nurses and orderlies—are they properly trained and are there enough of them? What of aides and workers—are they friendly and cooperative? And respectful? For instance, do they address the resident with dignity, calling the person Mr. ____, Mrs. ____, or Miss ____? Or is the patient patronizingly placed on a first-name basis? Nursing homes should foster a sense of hope and self-esteem, and small details like the respect accorded residents are vital in this regard.

Are medical records kept on the residents and is provision made for dental, eye, ear and foot care? Is there an affiliation or transfer arrangement with a nearby general hospital? Are there psychiatrists or psychologists on the staff and professionals in rehabilitation services for those who have had strokes or suffered broken bones?

Nursing homes almost without exception will conduct a complete physical examination of the aged person before or upon admission. The adult child will want to assure that an individual-treatment plan based on this examination is maintained by the nursing home.

• *Social Atmosphere*

No one places a parent in a nursing home with the idea that they should vegetate there. Thus it is important to inquire about group activities and recreational and educational programs available to the residents. How good is the library? Are lecturers brought in on occasion, and are there trips to the theater, to concerts, to museums for those who are up and about? What about wheelchair patients? Can they get out too?

Religion is of special concern to most older persons. Are religious services conducted regularly and for people of various persuasions? This is a matter to be inquired into particularly in instances of denominational nursing homes. Are clergy of other faiths welcome in the nursing home to minister to residents of different faiths?

What sort of volunteer program is operative at the nursing home, and does it exist to make the staff's work easier or the resident's stay more agreeable?

What about patients' rights? In 1973 the American Hospital Association drafted a bill of rights for hospital patients. A year later, the then-Department of Health, Education, and Welfare issued an equivalent bill detailing rights and responsibilities of long-term-care patients. Is a "Patient Bill of Rights" posted in the nursing home? By the same token, is there a patient or resident council for the airing of concerns, grievances, and recommendations? Is there a family organization where parallel cares and worries might be aired? Is there a family-support group? It is not only the person being placed in a nursing home who is challenged to adjust. Family members also frequently need help in dealing with reactions of a loved one to institutionalization. For the children of nursing home patients, individual counseling, group therapy, seminars, and other programs promoting direct involvement in the institution can be very helpful.

Finally, visiting hours. Are they generously scheduled, and to whom do they apply? For instance, are grandchildren and other young persons welcome? It is to be hoped that they are, if only to liven what can easily become a dull atmosphere.

Allow Proper Adjustment Time

Nursing home placement is a difficult experience—for the aged parent; for the adult children. All sorts of adjustments are required, and the most difficult of these are psychological. The parent may resent being placed in a home; the child may feel guilt for having placed the parent there. These feelings can give way to recriminations and complaints. The parent may accuse the child of lack of love and gratitude; the child in turn may turn on a home's administrators and cavil about the parent's room, the food, whatever.

Keep in mind that this is a hard time for everyone. Certainly it is possible to make a mistake about a particular nursing home, and certainly no one is happy about having to go into a nursing home. However, individuals are advised not to panic too soon and leap to "corrective" actions which might only result in the further complication of matters.

Gerontological professionals estimate that it can take as long as six months for an aged person to adjust to a nursing home. If mistakes have been made, they can be corrected. Meanwhile, presuming that careful thought went into the placement, the initial problems connected with the placement should be given time to work themselves out. The aged parents should be encouraged to adjust—and given time to adjust. There will be painful moments on both sides, but a thoughtful decision mutually arrived at should not be allowed to be undone by the emotionalism of the moment.

Alternatives to Nursing Homes

The British humor magazine *Punch* not long ago published a cartoon of several old couples in the parlor of a rather seedy nursing home. A man leans towards a crony and confides out of earshot of his wife: "We stayed together for the sake of the children, then the little buggers put us in the same home."

The cartoon was intended, of course, as a touch of sophisticated humor. But it also said volumes about the human condition, for many older persons live in dread of nursing homes, even the best of these homes. Faced with the loss of independence and other normalities of their long life, they feel panic and depression when the idea of institutionalization is broached. The very thought that they are surrendering their freedom and losing their independence, in whatever measure, is enough to fill many older people with despair.

For some aged persons there is no feasible alternative to a nursing home. The persons may be a safety risk to self and family, or mentally unstable, or otherwise so severely handicapped as to require 24-hour attention. On the other hand, for others it just may be that the move to a nursing home can be eliminated or at least postponed by appropriate care at home. Certainly several possibilites should be explored before the adult child judges an elderly parent unqualified to live any longer at home and institutionalizes that parent.

To begin with, it may be that the elderly parent's inability to function at home is caused by physical surroundings which can be changed. As Richard Griffin of the Cambridge (Massachusetts) Council on Aging comments, "Much more dependency than is commonly realized is environmental in character. By making changes in the physical environment at home or by having elderly people move to properly equipped buildings, one can sometimes make it possible for them to continue getting by on their own." For example, kitchens can be made safer for people with handicaps, such as those with defective vision; they face less danger from a stove whose controls are in front rather than in back behind the burners. Also, those unsteady on their feet will find security in bars installed on bathroom walls, and handrails built along hallways and stairways. "Architects are now learning to incorporate such safety features for older people in plans for new or rehabilitated housing," remarked Griffin. His message to adult children: Be alert about what might be done to make their aged parents' home or apartment safer.

Other alternatives to nursing homes:

Congregate housing. Residents of congregate housing receive help and encouragement from fellow residents and usually supportive services from a professional staff. Naturally, some places will be better than others, so they should be checked out carefully for safety, cleanliness, and conveniences. Maybe there will be losses of privacy, but these can be offset by advantages that would otherwise be missing from one's life. For instance, said Griffin, "There is no reason why older persons should have to prepare main meals individually. In congregate housing they don't have to. It can prove better psychologically and nutritionally to share the same meal with others in a common dining room."

Adult day care. This is a service particularly suited for aged persons living with adult daughters and sons who must go out to work, but who cannot leave aged parents unattended. The principle is similar to children's day care, the aged person spending all or part of the day at a center, then returning home for the night. The adult day-care center may be an independent support service, or it may be attached to a nursing home, clinic, or hospital (in which case it may be known as a day hospital). Some provide transportation; some feature medical, psychiatric, therapeutic, and nursing services; most will have recreational programs and hot meals. Adult day-care centers operate five days a week on a set schedule, like 9 a.m. to 5 p.m. They are not round-the-clock operations. Adult day care can be very effective. As Griffin declared: "It enables some elderly people who live in their own home to survive better by reason of the care they get five days a week at the center."

The availability of adult day care varies from community to community, as do funding sources and costs. A directory is available which provides an updated list of programs across the country. Requests for this adult day-care directory should be addressed to:

> Mrs. Edith G. Robins
> Special Assistant for Adult Day Health Services
> Division of Long Term Care, OSC
> Health Standards and Quality Bureau
> 1849 Gywnn Oak Avenue
> Baltimore, Maryland 21207

Officials at Beth Israel Hospital in Boston recommend adult day-care centers as having "particular applicability" to sufferers of Alzheimer's disease. (For more on Alzheimer's disease, see chapter 9.)

Foster home care. This is a relatively new concept, but it is one that seems certain to expand as the "old-old" population itself expands. (By the year 2000, it is estimated that the number of people over 75 will have increased by 60 percent from what it was in 1978.) The Massachusetts General Hospital initiated such a program five years ago, placing elderly patients whom it discharged in the homes of foster families who were paid $300 a month for expenses. Subsequently the Massachusetts legislature passed law authorizing money for the same purpose.

Off-and-on care. It may be that one's aged parent(s) need close attention and special care only during particular periods; for instance, during minor illnesses, after an accident from which the person is expected to recover, or in times of stress, as when a close friend dies. It is not necessary to consider nursing home placement on these occasions, and it may not even be necessary to move the parent(s) in distress into one's own home. Shared family responsibility, for which grandchildren and other relatives may be recruited, might resolve the care crisis. Family members might take turns sleeping over with the person in distress, or take turns visiting, performing chores, running errands until the temporary emergency is over.

A number of other public service and volunteer programs assist in enabling aged persons to stay living in their homes, rather than having to enter a nursing home or institutional facility. Some to keep in mind:

• *Meals-on-Wheels,* a Federally funded nutrition program, through which hot meals are delivered, usually once daily, to aged persons who have difficulty leaving their homes.

• *Day Activities Centers* and *Multiservice Centers for the Elderly,* which offer services ranging from handicraft and cooking classes, in the former instance, to health and dental screening and legal counseling in the latter.

• *Dial-a-Ride,* a transportation program for those aged parents who would otherwise be unable to get out to keep appointments or reach other destinations.

• *Friendly Visiting,* a program in which individuals look in on a household on a regular basis.

• *Chore Services,* a program where people will come into a house to do heavy-duty work, such as repairing a broken pipe or replacing a smashed pane of window glass.

• *Senior Citizen Centers,* places to get out to, where aged persons can enjoy the company of peers, join in recreational activities, and perhaps avail themselves of health and nutritional services.

• *Nutritional Centers,* a Federally funded program providing a hot noontime meal to the elderly, often in a church auditorium or school cafeteria.

• *Grandma and Grandpa Sitting Service,* a program whereby persons will come in and sit with an elderly person, keep the aged person company, read to him or her, etc. These programs are frequently found in college communities and are centered about young people anxious to do volunteer work or be sitters in return for an hourly fee.

• *Home Health Agencies,* a variety of offices and departments providing services to the elderly in their homes, and also information about paraprofessional services, such as practical nurses, home helpers, etc.

Not all these programs will be found in all communities, and in some communities many of these programs may be operative under different title designations than given here. By the same token, in some communities there may be still other programs than those listed above. Local councils on aging or the specialist in matters concerning the aged seated in virtually every city and town hall will be able to furnish details. Adult children are advised to check carefully with them on available services before making a decision on nursing home placement for an aged parent. It just may be that local programs will be found that will make it unnecessary to turn to a nursing home.

Death and Grief

Death is not a particular preoccupation with older people, popular mythology notwithstanding. When death is imminent, however, it triggers a series of reactions in the dying person, the range of which those close to the person should be acquainted with in order to cope with them. Dr. Elisabeth Kübler-Ross identified five stages of dying in her landmark study *On Death and Dying* (New York, 1969), and though it is still uncertain whether her five stages are fixed and changeless or social phenomena of the times and the culture, they are nevertheless generally accepted as typical for our moment of history. Kübler-Ross's stages of dying are these:

Denial ("I'm perfectly fine. The doctor doesn't know what he's talking about.")

Anger ("Why does everything have to happen to me? What did I do to deserve this?")

Bargaining (The most obvious form of bargaining is religious: "God, if you make me better, I won't drink for the rest of my life." Bargaining may also take the form of immersion in fitness programs, special diets, or search for that forever elusive magic elixir of life.)

Depression ("What have I got to live for? There's no point in struggling anymore.")

Acceptance ("Well, I've had a good life, and everyone has to go sometime. I'm ready any time the Lord wants me.")

How does the adult child help his or her aged parent through these stages of dying?

The first prerequisite is frankness and honesty—not a brutal frankness and honesty, but rather a gentle truthfulness about the facts of the parent's condition. An aged parent who is 75 has as much right to know his or her condition as a person who is 45. If the parent is disoriented or demented, then a certain caution might be dictated. The same with a parent who suffers a nervous disorder and may be unable to handle the reality of his or her own life. But on the whole, most persons want to know what is wrong with them, and it is kinder by far to tell them than to leave them puzzling in the dark. It is also the psychologically correct thing to do, as it can settle doubts, anxieties, confusions.

A second step is to avoid the extremes of unrealistic optimism and pessimistic confrontation. In the denial stage, for instance, it is very easy to become argumentative and confrontive, as with a parent who experiences chest pains but refuses to see a doctor. In cases of this sort a little gentle persuasion is far better than some shouted warning, 'You'll be dead next week, if you don't do something about yourself.' Confrontation may only harden the determination of the parent to be his or her own doctor.

Third, though it is important that one's parent be aware of his or her condition and have an idea of its implications, it is not necessary to go into morbid detail or to keep alluding to it. The ailing parent will provide most of the openings necessary for preparing for eventualities, particularly in the early phases of the illness. The adult child should beware hovering about like some kind of angel of doom.

Finally, the adult child should not be too quick in consigning the parent to the grave. Stories abound of the aged woman who beat cancer and the old man who beat a heart attack and went on to longer and continued fruitful life. Similarly, realize that the diagnosis made may not be the one to carry the aged parent off. Mother's cancer may go into remission, and it is probably the heart that will do her in—eight years from now.

In a word, be prepared for surprises; life does not always follow the script we would write for it. And be prepared too to discover that the stages of grief through which one's dying parent passes may also be experienced by you, the adult child. The adult child in turn can become overwhelmed by denial, anger, depression. The adult child may also be given to do some bargaining. Once again, the objective is to work through these stages to acceptance—acceptance that this is the reality of the situation. For only then can the facts be dealt with in a truly practical way.

Chapter 9

ALZHEIMER'S DISEASE

"The Disease of the Century"

ALZHEIMER'S disease has been termed "the disease of the century" by Dr. Lewis Thomas, science writer and chancellor of the Memorial Sloan-Kettering Cancer Center in New York, because in his words "of all the health problems in the 20th century, this one is the worst." It is not an uncommon illness, researchers estimating that 75 percent of all dementia patients are suffering from it. That translates to hundreds of thousands of Americans, since of the 25 million Americans over age 65, some 6 percent suffer from severe dementia. An additional 10 percent are estimated to be mildly to moderately so troubled. The figures are those of the National Institute on Aging. The American Association of Retired Persons says that Alzheimer's disease affects close to 1.2 million persons over the age of 65, and 60,000 under 65.

Yet, though the disease afflicts so many and though doctors have known about it for a long time (its symptoms were first described in 1906 by Dr. Alois Alzheimer), it is only recently that the illness has gripped the public consciousness in a decisive way. It has done so largely through articles appearing in the popular print media. Nevertheless, when a family is told that a parent or relative has Alzheimer's disease, family members have considerable difficulty finding material on the illness and its consequences. Presently, most of the material is ephemeral in nature—a newspaper or magazine article, a television report. You remember it, you look back for it, and it is gone, fled like yesterday's news. Example: the segment of ABC's "20—20" program for June 23, 1983, featuring Barbara Walters interviewing Yasmin Khan, the daughter of the one-time movie star Rita Hayworth. At 64, Rita Hayworth is in the last stages of Alzheimer's.

Because so little is concretely available, and because Alzheimer's disease is becoming such a particular family problem, the subject is pursued in detail in this book. The information here is derived from *A Family Handbook on Alzheimer's Disease and Related Disorders,* prepared by the Behavioral Neurology Unit at Boston's Beth Israel Hospital. Beth Israel is one of the three primary teaching hospitals of the Harvard Medical School. The other two are Peter Bent Brigham Hospital and Massachusetts General Hospital. The physician staffs at these hospitals hold simultaneous academic appointment at Harvard. The Behavioral Neurology Unit's handbook is intended to help families understand better what is happening to their loved one, and, equally urgent, what to expect as Alzheimer's disease progresses in the individual. Minor stylistic changes have been introduced into the Beth Israel handbook for purposes of this book, but in the main the sections are reproduced as they appear in the handbook.

Just What Is Alzheimer's?

Alzheimer's disease is not a psychiatric illness, but rather a neurological illness with abnormalities in the chemistry of the brain and changes in the structure of brain cells.

These changes cannot be seen on an x-ray, but only when brain tissue is examined under a microscope. Thus, Alzheimer's disease impairs brain function not because holes are produced in the brain but because structural and chemical changes prevent the nerve cells from functioning properly. In the beginning of the disease, relatively few brain cells are affected. As the disease progresses and abnormalities become more widespread, the behavior of patients becomes increasingly impaired. The spread of abnormal brain cells eventually hinders patients in performing simple everyday tasks such a feeding and dressing. They thus become less physically active and thereby more prone to other diseases such as pneumonia, which eventually lead to death. The rate of decline appears to vary greatly from person to person. At present, experts estimate life span after diagnosis to be five to ten years. Keeping the patient physically and mentally active definitely promotes better general health and may extend life-span as well.

The cause of Alzheimer's disease is currently unknown. Researchers are evaluating numerous possibilities, among which are the reduction of a special brain chemical, the increased accumulation of certain metals in the brain, and abnormalities in the system which makes us immune to disease. Many treatments are currently being tried, but no one has, as yet, found a cure. Particular dietary habits, professional occupations, or personality types do not seem to lead to developing Alzheimer's disease. However, heredity may play a role. Individuals with a family history of Alzheimer's disease are more likely to develop the illness than members of the general population, but that chance is still quite low. A very small number of Alzheimer's patients have what is called "familial Alzheimer's disease." These individuals come from families where as many as half of their relatives develop Alzheimer's disease. Fortunately, this form of the disorder is rare.

The earliest symptom of Alzheimer's disease is generally a subtle memory impairment such as forgetfulness. Family members may sense a difference in the person, but the difference is hard to pinpoint, especially since patients with Alzheimer's disease are often physically quite healthy. People commonly assume that the changes they see result from normal aging. While forgetfulness may occur as people grow older, in healthy individuals it does not interfere with their capacity to function or get progressively worse. Serious memory problems are not normal in the elderly and should be considered a sign of disease.

No one test can diagnose Alzheimer's disease. Instead, a thorough physical, neurological, and pyschiatric evaluation is necessary. A neurological examination detects the presence or absence of disease that affects the nervous system. Some tests of intellectual function will usually be performed. A psychiatrist should see the patient, since psychiatric illnesses, such as depression, resemble the symptoms of Alzheimer's disease. Standard medical tests also aid in the diagnosis of Alzheimer's disease. They will rule out other treatable diseases that might cause intellectual loss, such as brain tumors, drug reactions, and abnormal hormone function. The patient must have numerous blood tests as well as CT scans of the brain, and electrical measurements of the brain called EEG's. Special studies of the spinal fluid may also be performed. No one should accept the diagnosis of Alzheimer's disease without such a medical work-up.

After the diagnosis is made, the patient should be under the care of a physician. Since Alzheimer's disease is only beginning to be well understood, select a physician experienced in treating such patients. The physician can make recommendations regarding diet, sleep, mood, physical activity, and general health care.

Changes in Thinking Abilities

To understand the patient with Alzheimer's disease, one must understand the changes in thinking abilities that occur. A person's ability to think properly depends upon five major areas of intellectual activity: attention, memory, language, spatial orientation, and abstract reasoning. At one time or another Alzheimer's disease attacks all of these functions, but in the early stages of the disease only one or two of these abilities are usually affected while the others remain fairly normal.

Although the first symptoms of the disease vary, memory problems are the most common. Patients have particular difficulty learning new information. At first there is mild forgetfulness such as forgetting an appointment or a chore to be done. As memory problems become more severe, patients may start repeating themselves because they have forgotten what they have just said. Individuals may become disoriented or confused because they can't remember from moment and moment where they are or what they are doing. Eventually patients have difficulty remembering even very familiar situations and people.

While the ability to read may remain intact for a relatively long period of time, other language functions may be affected early in the disease. Patients have trouble finding the right words to express their ideas, causing hesitation or slowness of speech. Sometimes a person will substitute a word that is close in sound or meaning for the word he or she really wants to say. For example, when looking at a bench, the person may say "bunch" or "sofa." When quite pronounced, this problem will interfere with simple communication. When people have trouble communicating verbally, others find it hard to know what they are thinking. Remember that patients are often more aware of what is going on than they are capable of expressing. Since patients can often read even in fairly advanced stages of the disease, effective communication can continue through writing notes or instructions.

If individuals have difficulty with spatial orientation, this affects their ability to recognize people or see objects. Early in the disease, this is often mistaken for poor vision and patients try to find glasses to correct their visual problems. Tasks that require spatial judgment, such as putting a puzzle together, assembling a bicycle or building a bookcase present particular problems. Patients may get lost when driving because of this spatial disorientation. They may have trouble handling familiar objects, for example, trying to write with the wrong end of the pencil or putting their clothes on incorrectly. Eventually, even walking may present difficulties.

The ability to reason, plan ahead, and use sound judgment requires the complex interaction of many abilities and are thus often disturbed in patients with Alzheimer's disease. A simple task, such a wiping a table, may be carried out well, but tasks that require several steps, such as preparing a meal, may be disturbed. Individuals often appear to act impulsively because they have difficulty appreciating the interactions of events and thus the consequences of their actions.

All mental abilities suffer if a person has trouble paying attention or concentrating. As Alzheimer's disease progresses, patients experience particular problems in this sphere. They may begin a task, be distracted by something, and never complete it. They may ask a question but not hear the answer because their attention has wandered. They find it particularly hard to concentrate when other activities are going on. Thus, being among large numbers of people can exaggerate impairments.

Changes in Personality

Personality changes also occur among patients with Alzheimer's disease. The term personality refers to a person's unique behavior patterns; patterns that are consistent over time and across many different situations. In the early stages, according to Boston's Beth Israel Hospital's handbook, only slight changes in personality and behavior occur. Characteristic ways of responding that the individual has demonstrated throughout his life remain basically the same. As the disease progresses, however, personality and behavior changes can be expected to occur. The personality changes associated with Alzheimer's disease primarily result from two factors: 1) the structural and chemical changes in the brain produced by the disease; 2) emotional reactions to the consequences of the disease.

Brain changes appear to produce numerous alterations in personality. The Alzheimer's patient may fail to show initiative in daily activities and seem more withdrawn. Some patients are more easily agitated than prior to the onset of disease. Others become slightly inappropriate in social situations and appear tactless and impolite.

Depression occurs frequently in Alzheimer's patients. While biochemical changes related to the disease may cause, depression, it may also result from an emotional response to diminishing ability such as increased physical limitation, memory loss, and inability to perform routine tasks. In this sense, the response resembles that of other disabling diseases, such as arthritis or cancer. However, those diseases produce physical disabilities which remind us of their potential for producing emotional change. Alzheimer's disease causes no obvious physical alteration. The patient's appearance will not indicate that they have a memory problem or difficulty expressing themselves. Alzheimer's patients may fear that others will misinterpret their problems as mental retardation or psychiatric illness. They may be embarrassed or ashamed of their deficits because they feel others will not understand that they are the result of disease. Such patients withdraw from social situations, leaving them isolated and alone.

The memory problems experienced by the Alzheimer patient produce difficulties beyond the anxiety and frustration of forgetfulness. Patients who have misplaced something may suspect others of taking it. Similarly, if a social occasion seems to occur suddenly to the patient because plans have been forgotten, the patient may conclude that people are planning things behind his or her back. These difficulties can be minimized by reminding the patient about coming events and organizing the environment as suggested in the following section on home management. If personality changes become extreme or disruptive to daily living, the patient's physician may suggest medication or environmental changes which can improve the patient's outlook and maximize his level of functioning.

Helping the Patient at Home

Clearly, problems in thinking abilities can interfere with an Alzheimer patient's emotional well-being, safety, sense of orientation, communication, and activities of daily living. While there is presently no known way to restore normal functioning to your family member, there are many

ways to modify the patient's physical and social environment to fit his or her capacities and, at the same time, minimize stresses that difficulties evoke. However, each patient is different, so not all suggestions are appropriate for
any one person. Different functions can be affected at different times. Two basic techniques generally help the patient to function as independently as possible. First, adjust
the environment so that the person with Alzheimer's can
interact with it in a more organized and effective way.
Second, have family members give the patient assistance
whenever necessary.

Orientation. The patient may experience difficulty determining where he or she is or knowing the time of day, or
the day of the year.

Also, warns the Boston Beth Israel handbook, the person suffering Alzheimer's may fail to recognize a familiar
face, even that of a close relation. These and similar problems of orientation, can create embarrassment, frustration, and stress for both the patient and family members.

Perhaps the most important technique in preserving
orientation and the overall management of the patient is
creating a home environment which is *simply, orderly,* and
predictable, yet also allows freedom of movement. The
more variability in the patient's surroundings, the more
likely it is that he or she will become confused and disoriented. One room, or portion of a room, modified to the
needs of the patient as an "orientation area" will help
create simplicity and order in the home environment. The
best room is one that is centrally located and easily accessi-
ble. The orientation area should have a clock (perhaps
digital), a calendar, and a bulletin board or slate; thus providing a means for keeping track of the date and important

messages. A daily schedule of activities for the patient and for family members should be posted to assist the patient in remembering what to do when and in knowing where family members are at all times. Labeled pictures of family members, close friends, or pets will help the patient associate names with faces (brother, John; our cat, Sigmund). Items essential to the patient for daily living activities, such as eyeglasses, keys, and writing accessories might be placed in this area.

Thus, the orientation area can serve as a focal location in which the patient can find orientation clues, specific information, and items needed in the course of a day. This minimizes the number of trips around the house that produce disorientation, while at the same time it maximizes the efficiency of searching.

Structure can be imposed in the remaining portions of the house by labeling drawers, closets, or rooms. Avoid changing the arrangement of furniture, color schemes, or anything else that will reduce the familiarity of the surroundings.

In addition to such permanent aids, it is very helpful for family members to provide moment-to-moment cues for the patient. For example, upon awakening, one might say, "Oh George, what beautiful summer weather we are having this Tuesday." This type of cueing is particularly helpful outside the home. "We are at the post office to buy some stamps and to mail a letter to our son, Fred." Also, tell the patient in advance what is scheduled for the day; where he or she is going, with whom, and for how long. Reviewing these activities upon their completion will also be of benefit. "We are done buying stamps and mailing the letter to our son, Fred."

Keep in mind that these strategies can be successfully applied to most activities of daily living. Such approaches will help maintain desired behaviors and enable the patient to function as efficiently and independently as possible. However, one should remember that the patient can only function within the limits of his abilities and, since these are likely to decline over time, adjustments in management must be made accordingly.

Activities of Daily Living

Some useful techniques for common activities of daily living are described in this section. Since each patient is different, one may have to make some modifications. In general, keeping daily activities scheduled at the same time each day will add a degree of predictability to the patient's environment.

Washing and Grooming. Reduce activities in the bathroom to an easy and orderly sequence. Designate a shelf for the patient's use and label and arrange the accessories used for washing and grooming in the order they are to be used. To remind the patient where to return each accessory, the shape of each one can be outlined on the surface of the shelf with waterproof tape or ink. Labeling sink valves and removing all unnecessary or potentially dangerous instruments reduces the probablity of injury. If necessary, someone should check on water level and temperatures for bathing. Also consider installing slip-proof surfaces in the shower or bath, mounting support handles and rails, or installing a bath bench.

Eating. One may notice slight changes in the patient's diet. The patient's tastes and ability to eat certain foods vary with time. The family should recognize and adjust to such changes in food preferences but at the same time make sure the patient receives a balanced diet.

Medications. It is likely that your family member will receive a variety of medications. For some patients, a daily reminder ensures that the medication will be taken. However, if the patient cannot manage his or her medication, the family must assume responsibility. If the patient will be alone when medication is to be taken, prepare single doses in advance with the appropriate instructions. These might be placed in the orientation area. Alternatively, a neighbor can help by dropping in when it is time for the medication to be taken.

Personal Belongings. Whenever possible, keep frequently used personal belongings in the orientation area. A label, and perhaps an outline of the object marked on a shelf in the area, increases the chance of its being returned and easily located the next time. If necessary, have the patient practice placing the item over its outline. Misplacing eyeglasses is a common problem. If eyeglasses cannot be kept in the orientation area, especially if they are worn fairly often, the patient can wear them around his neck on a strap or chain. While some patients complain that the strap is unattractive, remember that this technique spares the frequent disruption of a house search.

Finances. This issue may threaten the patient. At some point, however, one must decide whether the patient should handle his or her own finances. At that time, legal advice may help determine if financial responsibility should be shifted to another family member.

Driving. Many patients successfully drive automobiles in the early stages of the disease. However, this activity should be monitored closely. At some point the patient may become lost, especially in unfamiliar places, or fail to respond to traffic signals. The family must then decide whether the patient should continue driving. Since withdrawing the privilege of driving may be a sensitive issue, the decision should come from a physician.

Exercise. Exercise is essential for good health in all individuals and particularly the patient with Alzheimer's disease. Exercise also relieves tension. Incorporate exercise, such as walking or bicycling, into your family member's daily routine, scheduling it at the same time each day. Exercise with him or her, if you can or must.

Recreation. The patient with Alzheimer's disease may still participate in games and other activities but only in new ways. The patient may, for example, be able to play golf but not keep score. On the other hand, less complex activities that require shorter attention span may be more enjoyable. Listening to familiar music is often an enjoyable recreational activity for patients. This can conjure up pleasant memories about events, places, and people of the past.

Communication. Patients with Alzheimer's disease often have trouble with conversation. Poor concentration is one source of difficulty. Your family member may have particular problems if more than one person is speaking. Try to be sure you have his or her attention. Call him or her by name. Let the person see your face as you talk. Hearing is easier when looking at the person who is talking. Reduce or eliminate competing sounds. For example, turn down the TV or radio; if there is noise in the next room, close the door to shut it out. Reduce the length of time listening is required. The patient may be able to concentrate well for a short period of time, then, after a period of rest, may be ready to concentrate again.

The Alzheimer's patient may have difficulty understanding what he or she hears. The patient hears words but does not understand them. Speak slower than usual. Repeat or reword what you have said when it is not understood. Use normal facial expressions and gestures to accompany what you say. The patient's seeing, as well as listening, helps him or her to understand.

If your relative has trouble remembering what has been heard, simply remind him or her of the information. Write down vital information, and post it on the bulletin board in the orientation area.

What is being said may be too difficult for the patient to grasp. The patient may follow one-step directions (such as, "Turn the light on, please."), but have trouble with multi-step directions (such as, "Please put the magazine away and then help me set the table.") For multi-step directions, give one step at a time. After each step is done, give the next one. If the patient has trouble listening to more complicated information, such as a news report, review the information, breaking it down into terms that he or she can follow. Routine family-oriented conversation is highly recommended. It will interest the patient and, because of its familiarity, should be easier to follow.

Your family member may not be able to choose words or pronounce them as well as in the past. If he or she has trouble talking, try to get the gist of what he or she is saying. If you have an idea of what is trying to be said, ask: "Do you mean _____?" You may need to try several possibilities before determining the message. If you do not know what he or she is trying to say, ask the person to give the message in another way. Encourage the patient to use an alternative word or gesture. Consider writing: "I don't know what you mean. Tell me again." Be patient. Allow the patient time to express himself or herself.

If your family member has trouble remembering what he or she has said, remind the person of the information if it is important. If he or she repeats himself or herself, it is best not to say anything about it. He or she may only feel embarrassed and frustrated unnecessarily.

If your relative hears better when you talk louder, the person may be experiencing a hearing loss. If you suspect that this may be the case, bring the patient for an ear examination to a physician who specializes in ear, nose, and throat problems, and an audiologist (one who tests hearing). These two specialists generally work together in the same office, clinic, or hospital. A hearing loss might be treatable.

Do not feel limited to the suggestions here. By all means, feel free to use your own ingenuity. Many methods may seem childish or tedious, but if they help to maintain the patient's well-being, they will be of benefit to all concerned.

The Family's Response

Although the patient's changes and losses are the first area of concern, it is also important to understand how Alzheimer's disease affects the whole family. Any illness creates stress and change in a family system. Certain themes, difficulties, and reactions are common to families caring for a family member with Alzheimer's disease. However, since each patient is unique and every family is different, there.will be variations in how each family comes to grips with the difficult situations it faces.

Family members experience many reactions as they care for a loved one with Alzheimer's disease. Difficult decisions are made that will profoundly affect the patient and the family. In the face of this stressful situation, caretakers may become aware of strong feelings or may notice changes in their own behavior and activites. These feelings are normal and natural responses to a difficult situation. At times it is useful to share these feelings with a mental health professional who has experience in the area of dementia. Your physician might know of a qualified social worker, psychologist, or psychiatrist. Family service agencies usually can provide this kind of assistance.

Emotional Response

Families caring for a patient with a chronic illness such as Alzheimer's disease frequently experience periods of depression. Sometimes caretakers feel sorry for themselves, while at other moments their sadness is for the patient. A healthy spouse may feel as though he or she lacks the energy needed to socialize or to pursue activities that were once meaningful. In response to the new emotional and physical demands, the caretaker's appetite or sleep habits may change. Family members worry about what the future holds for the patient and for themselves. Family members are sometimes surprised at the angry feelings that periodically emerge as they care for the patient. They wonder how they can feel angry with someone they love who is sick. Frustration and anger in this kind of situation are normal feelings. The patient exhibits irritating behavior at times. The patient seems ungrateful for the care that is provided. The patient's illness seem unfair. A husband or wife may feel deserted by the patient at a time in life when companionship seems so important.

Caretakers experience guilt in response to these conflicting feelings. They wonder if they have done everything possible for the patient. Guilt may arise over misunderstanding that one had with the patient in the past. One must recognize that any close relationship that endures over many years will have many aspects to it. The stress

created by an illness touches every member of the family.
The illness affects each family member differently and
changes its effect on that person from time to time. Only
one thing is certain. New emotions will be felt and these
changes are normal. Reaching out for help will better
enable the family to cope and remain intact.

Role Changes

Roles form the basis for human relationships and interactions. Society defines the expected behavior and responsibilities that people will assume in their various roles.
Over the years we grow comfortable in our own specific
roles and come to depend on others for fulfilling the roles
that they play. In a family we learn to rely on each other
for certain things. For example, a family may look to
Grandma to organize and make preparations for the large
gathering each year at Thanksgiving. A wife may count on
her husband to make financial and investment decisions.
An adult child still turns to his aging parents for advice and
emotional support. Sadly, the intellectual, behavioral, or
emotional changes that accompany Alzheimer's disease
can alter the patient's ability to function in his or her accustomed role. The family, recognizing these changes,
must make adjustments.

To understand fully the changes in roles, one must appreciate the loss experienced both by the patient and by the
family. If Grandma has been accustomed to running the
household for many years, the realization that others are
now called on to perform these tasks may upset her. If it is
the husband who must learn to assume some of these new
responsibilities, he may be understandably anxious, angry,
or sad about the situation in which he now finds himself.
Sometimes the illness makes it impractical for a patient to

continue working, resulting in an unplanned and early retirement and financial strains. The patient with Alzheimer's disease and his or her family will experience many adjustments and changes. Understandably, patients and families experience a mixture of emotions including sadness, anger, and anxiety. The family must cope with many losses. The family should work to create effective strategies which compensate for the losses.

Difficulties in Social Situations

Families usually attempt to protect the patient with Alzheimer's disease in social situations. In the early stages of the illness, the patient may be unable to converse as heretofore or may forget and repeat a story. Family and friends often try to "cover up" for the patient's diminished social skills. They may fill in missing words for the patient or divert the focus of attention away from him or her. Experiencing a sense of discomfort or embarrassment for the patient is normal. Families are often uncertain about how to deal with this problem. Is it best to isolate the patient so that difficult situations are avoided? Should the patient and family continue with social lives as if nothing had changed? Unfortunately, no easy answer exists. One might begin by asking the patient what he or she would like. Some situations may now be more stressful than others for the patient. For example, Grandpa may state that he continues to enjoy weekend family gatherings that include his children and grandchildren, but finds the weekly card games are "just too much." The goal should be to keep the patient as socially active as possible. Social isolation and exclusion may lead to a lower level of functioning or increased confusion.

Another issue that confronts all families in this situation

is how to explain the patient's illness to others. A young child may not understand why his grandmother does not recognize him. Friends may be confused about why the patient and his wife no longer go to social gatherings as often as in the past. Some friends and family have trouble viewing the patient as "sick" since the patient with Alzheimer's disease often appears physically healthy. The explanation of the illness that one gives to family and friends will vary; there are no "right" or "wrong" answers. Some families feel it is important to emphasize that the patient has a neurological illness, in contrast to a psychiatric disorder. In general, a truthful and simple explanation will suffice.

Young children need to know that the patient's behavior is not a reflection on anything they have done. For instance, if children understand that Grandpa is sick, they are less likely to feel that Grandpa does not remember their names because he does not love them. If one wants to enlist the aid of neighbors in the care of the patient, they can be more helpful once they have a clear understanding of the problem. In new social situations, everyone may feel more relaxed if they understand ahead of time what the patient's difficulties are and how they can make the situation most comfortable for him or her. In dealing with the patient who has Alzheimer's disease, the family can benefit from all the emotional and practical support that is available around them. A basic understanding of the patient's illness will allow those who want to help to come forth. The patient benefits, as does the family.

The husband and wife of the patient with Alzheimer's disease must face some alterations in his or her social world. The healthy spouse may realize that some acquaintances visit less frequently. The patient may no longer enjoy going out on weekends to a play or a movie. He or she may be less affectionate than previously. The patient's doctor often suggests that frequent travel to new places is disruptive for the patient and should be avoided. How is the patient's spouse supposed to react to these changes? Once again, we are faced with a difficult situation that does not have just one correct solution. Each spouse must develop a comfortable strategy for himself or herself. The continuing needs of the healthy spouse for social involvement are important. If the patient feels uncomfortable about an activity, the spouse need not sacrifice it totally. Perhaps a friend or family member can join the healthy spouse for an occasional movie matinee or evening out. Make plans, as needed, to have someone stay with the patient on these occasions. We all need time for work *and* time for leisure, particularly the spouse of the patient with Alzheimer's disease. These needs are healthy and normal. Periods of time away from the patient can re-energize the family member, allowing the person to continue caring for the patient.

People experience the desire to give and receive love in different ways at each stage of life. Sadly, changes in the emotional state of the Alzheimer's patient may affect the capacity to give and receive love. The patient who was once sensitive and thoughtful in relationships with family and friends may become more preoccupied with his or her own needs. The wife or husband, working so hard to provide for the patient's needs may feel angry that there is no expression of thanks. The patient may forget a birthday or anniversary. Do not view these changes in the patient as a reflection on something one might have done, said or felt. Rather, these changes are part of the illness.

The social alterations are probably the most difficult aspect of the illness for families to face. The patient's lost social abilities may make those who love him feel the saddest. This is understandable, since the way one views, comes to know, and grows to love others is largely based on their social traits—their sense of humor, their kindness, their special interests. Those who are closest to the patient may experience a strong mixture of feelings as they face the patient's changes in these spheres. Talking with a professional about the impact of these alterations in the patient may help. Certainly families and friends should draw together to provide mutual support. When the burden of care is shared, the task is far more bearable.

The Question of a Nursing Home

Many families agonize over the decision to seek an appropriate nursing home for the patient. Husbands, wives, or adult children who have worked to keep the patient at home may feel a sense of failure and guilt when they begin to wonder about nursing homes. Each family's ability to maintain the patient at home is different. The level of functioning varies from patient to patient. The availability of community resources differs widely. The health and energy levels of family members to provide care will vary. Because of all of these factors, no fixed guidelines can dictate when a patient needs nursing home care, according to the Beth Israel Hospital handbook.

One important factor for families to consider is the patient's safety. If staying at home without supervision is dangerous to the patient, alternatives should be considered. For example, if a patient lives alone and begins to forget to turn off the gas jets of the stove, the family needs to consider the patient's well-being. The health of the caretaker or spouse also affects decisions about keeping the patient at home. If the patient's demands begin to jeopardize or compromise the caretaker's health, other strategies for providing care should be explored. In planning for care, it is best to strike a balance that considers the patient's needs and the family's needs.

Some families find it useful to talk about nursing homes and even visit several facilities before a crisis arises. Just knowing that an alternative exists, if needed, allows some families to persevere at home. A nursing home may have a lengthy waiting list for admission. Certainly a nursing home placement requires careful planning. The financial arrangements for entry into a nursing home must be clearly understood. Programs such as Medicaid can help the patient with limited financial resouces who requires nursing home care. Applications for benefits may have to be filed. If the patient has assets and/or income, the family considering nursing home placement should understand the state laws that govern financial responsibility for and joint ownership of property. Generally, the patient is ineligible for state assistance until most of his or her assets have been depleted for medical care. Planning should involve and include the patient, the family, the patient's doctor or nurse, and a social worker who is knowledgeable about community resources.

Community Services

It should go without saying that the family providing care for someone with Alzheimer's disease should familiarize itself with services offered by community agencies— some of which are geared to meet the patient's need; some, the needs of the spouse and other family members. Services will vary from community to community, so no definitive, nation-wide itemization of what is available is possible. However, a professional counselor, social service

agency, or one's pastor or rabbi will be able to advise and
steer in proper directions. Boston's Beth Israel Hospital's
handbook lists several possibilities, all of which are sum-
marized below. I adopt the summary method to avoid
overlap with the subchapter "Alternatives to Nursing
Homes" in chapter 8. What follows should be read in con-
junction with that section of the book. The services cited in
Beth Israel's handbook:

• *Visiting Nurse Associations and Home Health Agencies.* Such agency programs provide the services of
registered nurses, therapists, nursing assistants, or home
health aides who may give injections, dispense medication,
or help the individual attend to personal hygiene, according to the attendant's professional qualifications. The
family is advised to inquire about costs for these services
and to check medical insurance policies about reimbursement coverage. Some policies require that the services be
ordered by the patient's doctor in order for reimbursement
to be made.

• *Homemakers, Home-Care Agencies.* These programs
enlist people, who come into the house to do light housekeeping, help with the grocery shopping, meal preparation, and the like. Costs vary according to the community,
and in some places there may be no cost at all for people
over 65 meeting certain criteria.

• *Adult Day Care.* This is a relatively new service, which
provides the patient with a structured day program outside
the home. The programs are geared to aid the patient in
such areas as nutrition, nursing, recreation, and socializa-
tion. This is a program which the Beth Israel handbook
says has "particular applicability to the Alzheimer's
disease patient."

• *Companions, Friendly Visitors.* These are persons who provide company and help to the Alzheimer patient, perhaps accompanying him or her on a medical appointment, perhaps just visiting on occasion. Companions and friendly visitors may be found through volunteer agencies, Home-Care agencies, religious groups, college student employment centers, advertisements in newspapers, or from among one's friends and neighbors. Warning: Choose the person with care and expect an adjustment period as the patient and companion get to know one another.

• *Transportation Services.* For reasons of safety, families must consider carefully whether an Alzheimer's patient should continue to drive. When driving does become impossible, a number of alternatives are available, even beyond public transportation. Various "handicap transportation" services exist; some hospitals maintain van service to transport patients to medical appointments; fraternal groups may have drivers at the ready. Check with City Hall or the community's Office on Aging.

• *Volunteer Groups.* A variety of organizations offer a variety of services in a variety of fields, but often must be ferreted out. United Way offices or one's area Red Cross office are good sources of information; so also City Hall, Senior Citizen Centers, churches, synagogues, and hospitals.

• *Financial Aid.* One's doctor or a social worker will know the appropriate agency to contact if one is in need of financial assistance, but the logical starting places for aid are the local welfare office (first-time visitors are advised to ask for an "intake worker"), the local Social Security office (particularly if one has been forced to stop working because of a disability), and the personnel department where one works or worked. Programs for financial assistance of course vary widely from place to place, as do the procedures for applying for aid and the criteria for being eligible for financial assistance.

• *Support Groups.* Families caring for patients often find it helpful to share their experiences and thoughts in a group setting. Support groups provide an opportunity for family members to come together with others in similar situations. Strategies on providing care can be exchanged in a group, problems can be raised, feelings can be aired, and medical information or research on Alzheimer's disease can be discussed. To locate such a support group, there are several places one might inquire. The physician treating the patient may know of support groups. One might call a local hospital and speak with a person in the Social Service Department. The local Department of Mental Health may have some suggestions. Finally, there is a newly formed Alzheimer's organization that has information on activities of 50 chapeters in 25 states. One can reach them by writing or phoning:

ADRDA/National
360 N. Michigan Avenue, Suite 601
Chicago, IL 60601

(312) 853-3060

Chapter 10

WHERE TO TURN

Support Programs

IN every community there are specific individuals in positions to offer advice, help, and counsel on problems involving the elderly. These resource people would be first and foremost the professional health-care officials and social workers. They would be doctors and church people: priests, ministers, rabbis. They might be knowledgeable neighbors—the druggist down the street; the couple across the way with aged parents for whom they are responsible. One should not be timid about approaching those in a position to convey the information which many of us never bother to assimilate until a crisis descends on us.

The wise person is the one who keeps abreast by reading newspapers, by subscribing to magazines concerned with aging, by checking out the literature in one's public library, including reference books such as the *Information Please Almanac,* which has an excellent section on growing older. Persons so doing will discover that a host of support programs exist for the long-term care of the aged, the majority of them focused on helping older persons maintain their independence in their homes and communities for as long as possible.

Many people carry a prejudice against certain public programs, since to them they smack of "welfare" in the old Depression-time, near derogatory use of the word. They are advised to regard such instincts as false or misplaced pride, and they should take advantage of all that their tax dollars have helped make possible in the caring society.

Following is a summary of the principal support programs available to Americans:

FEDERAL

Medicare (Title XVIII). This is a health-insurance program for people 65 or older, people of any age with permanent kidney failure, and certain other disabled people. Medicare has two parts: hospital insurance, which helps pay for in-patient hospital care and certain followup care after discharge, and medical insurance, which helps pay for doctor's services and many other medical services and items. Persons receiving Social Security benefits or retirement benefits under the railroad retirement system qualify for both. Coverage is not free, and not everyone is automatically enrolled in medical insurance. Detailed information is available from Social Security offices (listed under "Social Security Administration" in telephone books) or railroad retirement offices.

Hospice Care. As of November 1, 1983, Medicare coverage was extended to hospice care. Such care provides a combination of medical, social, and psychological services to cancer patients and other people with a life expectancy of six months or less. The intent of the program is to encourage hospice care as an alternative to more costly forms of treatment, such as intensive care in hospitals. Hospice programs emphasize home care and the alleviation of pain and suffering, rather than the cure of disease.

Supplemental Security Income (SSI). A program that pays monthly checks to aged, disabled, and blind persons with limited income and assets. Payments are provided on the basis of income and eligibility criteria and are not payments for specific services, as in the military or the work force. Persons may be eligible even if they never worked. Also, there is no strict age requirement. A disabled child under 18 may be eligible if the physical or mental impairment is comparable in severity to one that would prevent an adult from working and is expected to last at least 12 months or result in death. SSI recipients are likewise eligible for Medicaid and Title XX programs (see next section). Further information is available from one's local Social Security office.

Veterans Administration (VA). The VA provides several types of long-term care for military veterans, including hospital and institutional care, contracted nursing care, and some home health care. These services are thought of primarily in terms of the veterans with a service-connected disability, but any veteran age 65 is eligible for care, no questions asked. In other words, once 65, there are no requirements of means or origin of ailment; that is, whether the ailment is service-connected or not. In the next few years most of the 11.5-million veterans of World War II will turn 65, at which age they will automatically become eligible for free medical care at VA hospitals and clinics. This is a service benefit which not all families are aware of, and which could be especially important to people in straitened circumstances or without adequate medical insurance of their own.

FEDERAL/STATE PROGRAMS

Medicaid (Title XIX). This is a program for long-term care available under a combination of Federal and state funding for certain needy persons of all ages. Standards and eligibility, as well as the services themselves, vary from state to state. Care in skilled nursing facilities is a mandated basic service; care in intermediate care facilities an optional service. Home health-care services is also a covered service. The program is administered within Federal guidelines by local social service departments.

Title XX Social Services. This is a Federal-state cost sharing program under the Social Security Act which provides funds for services such as aid to families with dependent children, chore/homemaker services, adult day care and adult foster care.

Older Americans Act. This is a program dating from 1965 to channel Federal monies to the states to provide services for the elderly. The funds are allocated on the basis of the individual state's elderly population and are used for such projects as hot meals, congregate meals served in central locations, and home-delivered meals for the housebound (meals-on-wheels). There is no means test for recipients, although an effort is usually made to locate services of the Act in low-income areas.

Rehabilitation Programs. Although most often focused on younger people, vocational and other rehabilitation programs exist for the long-term treatment of the chronically ill elderly. Check local social service agencies.

Housing Services. Many of the public and subsidized housing programs of the U.S. Department of Housing and Urban Development (HUD) are intended for the elderly and feature conveniences such as ramps, proximity to shopping malls, etc.

PAID EMPLOYMENT

The U.S. Department of Labor offers paid employment to certain elderly persons through its Older American

Community Service Program. The employment is part-time, and comes under the following headings:

Operation Mainstream. A program in conservation and beautification projects administered by the Forest Service of the Department of Agriculture in some 20 states. Write: USDA Forest Service, Room 3243, South Agriculture Building, 12th and Independence Avenue S.W., Washington, D.C. 20250.

Green Thumb. A program in conservation, beautification, and community improvement for men who have a rural or farming background. Sponsored by the National Farmers Union in 24 states. Physical examination necessary. Write: Green Thumb, Inc., 1012 14th Street N.W., Washington, D.C. 20005.

Green Light. A related program for women in community service. Same address as Green Thumb.

Senior Aides. A program of work with community-service agencies in a variety of activities; e.g., child care, adult education, home-health, and homemaker services. Administered by the National Council of Senior Citizens in some 33 urban and rural areas. Write: National Council of Senior Citizens, 1511 K Street N.W., Washington, D.C. 20005.

Senior Community Aides. A program of work in public or private service programs, such as assisting in child-care centers, vocational rehabilitation classes, secretarial tasks, and building security. Sponsored by the National Retired Teachers Association and the American Association of Retired Persons in more than 30 cities. Write: NRTA/AARP, 1909 K Street N.W., Washington, D.C. 20036.

Senior Community Service Aides. A program of work in Social Security, state employment offices, public housing, libraries, hospitals, schools, etc., sponsored by the National Council on the Aging in about 20 urban and rural areas. Work would involve such tasks as escort services, homemaking, home repair, and outreach for information and referral. Write: National Council on the Aging, 1828 L Street N.W., Washington, D.C. 20036.

VOLUNTEER SERVICE

The independent Government program ACTION coordinates and administers a number of domestic and international volunteer activities sponsored by the Federal Government. Persons interested in any of the activities listed below should contact ACTION, 806 Connecticut Avenue N.W., Washington, D.C. 20525 (toll-free number: 1-800-424-8580):

Foster Grandparent. A program for men and women, 60 or older, with low incomes, who wish to work with children on a one-to-one basis four hours a day, five days a week. Small stipend.

Peace Corps. A program of two-years' service in developing countries, for which participants receive a monthly living allowance and, at the end of their service, a cumulative readjustment allowance.

Retired Senior Volunteer Program (RSVP). A program to involve people 60 or over in work with children and the handicapped, assisting other older persons, or helping in a variety of community activities according to their interests. Out-of-pocket expenses. (Interested parties may also contact their state office on the aging.)

Senior Companion. A program modeled on the Foster Grandparent Program but aimed at serving adults with special needs, including the elderly, in homes, nursing facilities, or institutions. Small stipend.

Service Corps of Retired Executives (SCORE). A program involving retired business executives in helping owners of small businesses and community organizations with their management problems. Out-of-pocket expenses. (Interested parties may also contact the regional or district office of the Small Business Administration.)

Volunteers in Service to America (VISTA). A program involving volunteers in work in urban ghettos, small towns, rural areas, Indian reservations, or wherever poverty exists in the United States. Service is for one year, though people may reenroll. Monthly living allowance is provided, as well as a cumulative monthly stipend payable upon completion of service.

International Executive Service Corps (IESC). An independent organization supported by government and nongovernment funds, which features overseas service by executives. Contact IESC, 545 Madison Avenue, New York, N.Y. 10022.

ORGANIZATIONS

Belonging to a local or national organization can be helpful in small ways (such as securing discounts) and large (such as keeping abreast of new Federal and state government programs). Most organizations for the elderly invite membership when a person turns 55, and joining is recommended, especially so if one's own parents are still living. Two parties keeping abreast are better than one, particularly given the frequency with which changes occur in matters relating to the elderly. Some major national organizations:

American Association of Retired Persons (AARP), 1909 K Street N.W., Washington, D.C. 20049 (largest association of older persons with 14 million members).

National Council of Senior Citizens (NCSC), 1511 K Street N.W., Washington, D.C. 20005.

Gray Panthers, 3635 Chestnut Street, Philadelphia, Pa., 19104.

National Association of Retired Federal Employees (NARFE), 1533 New Hampshire Avenue N.W., Washington, D.C. 20036.

Older Women's League Educational Fund, 3800 Harrison Street, Oakland, Calif. 94611 (For ages 50-64).

Action for Independent Maturity (AIM), 1909 K. Street N.W., Washington, D.C. 20049.

National Center of the Black Aged, 1730 M Street N.W., Suite 811, Washington, D.C. 20036.

Catholic Golden Age, 400 Lackawanna Avenue, Scranton, Pa. 18503 (Eligibility beginning at age 50).

Central Bureau for the Jewish Aged, 80 Fifth Avenue, New York, N.Y. 10011.

National Tenants Organization, Inc., Suite 548, 425 13th Street N.W., Washington, D.C. 20004.

The Oliver Wendell Holmes Association, 381 Park Avenue South, New York, N.Y. 10016 (for intellectual stimulation among the elderly).

Urban Elderly Coalition, c/o Office of Aging of New York City, 250 Broadway, New York, N.Y. 10007.

Continuing Education

It may be a truism, but once again, to stay alive mentally is to stay alive physically. Courses of continuing education are therefore strongly recommended for the elderly. Adult children are doing an important service when they encourage their parents to enroll in art classes available evenings at one's local high school, or, say, to take up a foreign language in the extension program of a nearby college or university. The intellectual stimulation and challenge will do them a world of good.

In this context, it is well to know of the Elderhostel movement. Elderhostels are relatively new, having their inception only in 1975. But they serve thousands, and have spread from the state of New Hampshire, where they began in five colleges, to more than 600 colleges, universities, independent schools, folk schools, and other educational institutions in the United States, Canada, Bermuda, Mexico, Great Britain, Scandinavia, Holland, France, Germany, and Italy. In 1983 it was projected that Elderhostel and its international network would serve 78,000 hostelers, an increase of 42 percent over 1982.

Elderhostels provide week-long educational experiences in the liberal (as distinct from gerontological) arts. Persons 60 years of age and over, or those whose participating spouse or companion qualifies, are welcome in the program. There are no previous-education requirements, and during the week local tours and recreational opportunities are arranged for the participants. Elderhostel weeks are scheduled for the spring and summer months, when campuses would be otherwise little used, or not used at all.

This is a sample Elderhostel Week, as offered at the University of New England in Biddeford, Maine, from June 12-18, 1983:

Program A — "The French Experience in New England," "The American West Through Artists' Eyes," "Let's Go to the Opera."

Program B — "Field Tripping in Maine," a course in natural history during which participants join in bird watching expeditions and visit nesting areas (including that of the bald eagle), trout hatchery, moose farm, etc.

Detailed information on Elderhostels and a catalogue of courses may be had by writing:

Elderhostel
100 Boylston Street
Boston, Massachusetts 02116

Incidentally, costs are purposefully kept low to accommodate the budgets of the senior generation, and there is a uniform maximum tuition for all Elderhostel Weeks. In 1983 the maximum weekly tuition charge was $180, with an additional $10 per week permitted for programs in Alaska and Hawaii. The charge is all-inclusive, and covers room and board, all classes, and a variety of extra-curricula activities.

Elderhostel Weeks are ideal for those looking for intellectual stimulation, those who like to travel, and those who are anxious to reach out for new experiences. Adult children who place their parents' names on the Elderhostel mailing list are doing them a great favor.

Chapter 11

TOWARDS THE FUTURE

Closing Statement

THE family is inevitably the locus of most social and intergenerational changes relating to aging. In recent years, however, many writers have been quick to toll the bell for the family as a stabilizing element in the society. Easy divorce, the dispersal of offspring, the concern with "me" as the most important person in my life (a la the television commercial featuring Jack Klugman)—factors such as these have spawned stories on the end of the family and, concomitantly, stories on America's neglected elderly. Now certainly the family has its problems, and certainly many of America's elderly are neglected. But the family remains the cornerstone it historically has been, and the family as we have known it does not seem particularly threatened as an institution, despite the forces at work on it. Its responsibilities remain firmly in place, including responsibilities to the elderly, as Raymond Johnson of the Wartburg Lutheran Home for the Aging argued they do earlier in the book. Though most older persons do not live with their children, in the vast number of cases this is by choice and is as it should be, all things considered.

Though most may not share a household with their adult children, still 84 percent of people 65 or older live less than an hour away from one of their children, and four out of five see an adult child as often as once a week; two-thirds as often as every day or two. These are the findings of sociologists Matilda White Riley and Ann Foner in their notable study *Aging and Society Vol. I: An Inventory of Research Findings* (New York, 1968). Inevitably, seeing one's adult children often means seeing one's grandchildren also. In one urban study, 58 percent of old persons saw both their adult children and grandchildren every day. Considering how many more may telephone or write a letter, this does not translate into a breakdown of the family or to neglect of the elderly on any epidemic or alarming scale.

Of course some families fall short of meeting the needs of their elder members, and these failures are the more painful when there is not a public program to compensate for them. The more obvious, too. But so often the source of the problem is not indifference and much less outright cruelty; so often it is a case of the family not knowing where to turn for effective assistance or refusing to turn for assistance out of some mistaken notion of pride. Neither is excusable—because of the easy availability of information in the former instance, and, in the latter, the right we all have and should feel to share in what our tax dollars have made possible.

The sum of all this is that the American family is hanging together remarkably well in spite of some dramatic and often disrupting social changes. This may not make growing older any more agreeable. As Ruth Rowe said, "Getting old is pure hell." But it promises to make it a lot less troublesome for most of us—adult children and aged parents.

One thing more: Presuming that the family survives as social institution, which it will, what adult children do today for their aged parents will likely be returned in kind in the future by their own children. The power of example is that great and that enduring.